AUSTIN

BEER

CAPITAL CITY
HISTORY ON TAP

BITCHBEER.ORG
FOREWORD BY DEBBIE CERDA

AMERICAN PALATE

Published by American Palate
A Division of The History Press
Charleston, SC 29403
www.historypress.net

Front cover: Photo taken by Sarah Kealing. *Back cover, top left*: Courtesy of Shaun Martin; *center*: Courtesy of Holly Aker; *right*: Courtesy of Caroline Wallace. *Bottom*: Austin mural photo by Sarah Kealing.

First published 2013

Manufactured in the United States

ISBN 978.1.62619.094.8

Library of Congress CIP data applied for.

Notice: The information in this book is true and complete to the best of our knowledge. It is offered without guarantee on the part of the author or The History Press. The author and The History Press disclaim all liability in connection with the use of this book.

CONTENTS

ACKNOWLEDGEMENTS

To all the amazing people who've helped us along the way, we'd like to thank you for your unwavering support and infinite wisdom and for sharing your beer with us.

Matt Abendschein, Jon Airheart, the Aker family, Steve Anderson, the Auber family, *Austin Beer Guide*, the Austin Food Bloggers' Alliance, Austin Homebrew Supply, the Austin Zealots, Mohamad Balaa, William Bearden, Shane Bordeau, Keith and Pam Bradley, Kevin Brand, Addie Broyles, Bush Baby Beer, Casey Carpenter, Amy Cartwright and everyone at Independence Brewing Company, Bill and Marge Cawthon, Christine Celis, Debbie Cerda, Craft Pride, Adam DeBower, Dan and Joelle Dewberry, Dave and Melissa Ebel, Forrest Elliott, Brad Farbstein, Juan Carlos Ferrer, Jason Freed, William Golden, Michael Graham, Terry and Vickie Greer, John Gross, Tristan Hallman, Scott and Paula Hallman, Josh and Meg Hare and everyone at Hops & Grain, Josh Horowitz, Sarah Kealing, Wes Kitten and the Beer Haul, Bryan Koroleski, Habeab Kurdi, La Condesa, the Library of Congress, Ivy Le, Alden Loredo, Mark Jensen and Austin Beer Garden Brewing Co., Jake and Monica Maddux, Corey and Angela Martin, Beverly Martin, Rick Martin, Brian Martin, Chip McElroy, Stephanie Meyers, the McCullough family, Mike McGovern, Mike Miller and everyone at the Austin History Center, Mowgli Aker, Joe Mohrfeld, Billy Murff and the team at Adelbert's Brewery, Chris Oglesby, Chris Orf, Jon Partridge, Brian "Swifty" Peters, Cary Prewitt, Zoey Provino, Region

C, Andrew Rinehart and Good Libations, Justin Rizza, Forrest and Diane Rogness and everyone at Rogness Brewing, John Rubio and the *Beerists* podcast crew, everyone at PorchingDrinking.com, Ben Sabel and the guys at Circle Brewing, Jim Sampson, Mark Schoppe, Suzy Schaffer, Steve and Rena Schrader, Jeff Stuffings and the whole Jester King Craft Brewery team, St. Edward's University Hilltop Views, Brian Smittle, Ben Sabin and the folks at Thirsty Planet Brewing Company, John Stecker and Dariush Griffin and 4th Tap Co-op, Kevin Sykes, Chip Tait, the Texas Carboys, the Texas Craft Brewers Guild, the Texas State Archives, Christen Thompson, Kathy Towns, the University of North Texas, the University Of Texas's Dolph Brisco Center for American History, Davis Tucker, Julia Turner, the Wallace family, Michael Waters and Uncle Billy's Brew and Que, Ellen Weed, Jordan Weeks, Joe White, Josh Wilson, Ty Wolosin, the Wood family, Jeff Young and the Black Star Co-op crew, Forrest and Patrick Clark and Marco Rodriguez from Zilker Brewing Co., Greg Zeschuk and the *Beer Diaries* team and Dave Wolfe for getting us on BeerPulse.com.

FOREWORD

When I was asked by *Bitch Beer* cofounder and blogger Caroline Wallace to write the foreword for *Austin Beer*, I was surprised yet honored. There are so many voices to share tales of the people and places that have shaped the history and culture of craft beer in Austin, many of which you will encounter in the following pages of this book.

Documenting the history and culture of craft beer in Austin has been long overdue. The authors of *Austin Beer* have dedicated extensive time and energy to provide a comprehensive, informative and engaging summary of the long history of craft beer in Austin.

I have wondered why I was asked to write this foreword. It could be because I've been involved in craft beer in some form or fashion since about the time the authors were born yet recognize that the passion for craft beer narrows the generational gap in our Austin community. Or perhaps it's because I empathize with the phenomenon of mansplaining that happens too often to women in the craft beer community. As I write this foreword, I savor the knowledge that for the first time in thirty years, a woman has won the Homebrewer of the Year Award at this year's National Homebrew Conference, with an entry in one of the most difficult categories: Lite American Lager.

My personal journey into the Austin beer scene actually started in Houston. I worked at the historic Ale House, a British pub and restaurant that featured more than 130 beers from across the United States as well as from around the world.

I'll never forget the historic night that I met brewmaster Pierre Celis.

The date was October 17, 1989, at a wholesalers' beer conference in downtown Houston. I attended with my boyfriend at the time, an award-winning homebrewer who also worked at the Ale House as bar manager. His plan to open his own brewpub whenever the Texas legislature would get around to legalizing brewpubs in Texas meant countless hours of research through pilot brews and beer tastings, and I was a willing assistant in the brew kitchen.

At the conference, we visited the hospitality suite hosted by C.R. Goodman Distributing, where we mingled with other beer industry representatives, including three generations of the Young Brewery dynasty.

At the time, C.R. Goodman had an association with Manneken-Brussels Imports and was the Texas distributor of Hoegaarden. I was already a fan of the Hoegaarden White Ale and was pleased that the infamous Verboden Vrucht (Forbidden Fruit) was available at the intimate gathering. (Due to the Renaissance nudes on the label, Forbidden Fruit was not approved for distribution in Texas.) At 8.5 percent alcohol by volume (ABV), it was my first intoxicating taste of a Belgian strong ale.

I was introduced to Pierre—the first professional brewer I'd ever met—and we conversed in French since he spoke very little English and I couldn't speak a lick of Flemish. He mentioned that C.R. Goodman was encouraging him to open a brewery in Texas. A few years later, Celis Brewery came to fruition in our capital city, and not long after, I moved to Austin.

I saw Pierre Celis again at a Celis Brewery event, and he recalled our initial meeting. By that time, Texas had legalized brewpubs, and I was bartending at Armadillo Brewing Company on Sixth Street and drinking fabulous craft beers at the various other brewpubs downtown.

As that initial wave of brewpubs waned, the limited yet dedicated brewers and founders of Live Oak and Real Ale, as well as "latecomer" Independence Brewing, worked long hours with limited staff to survive and succeed, setting the foundation for the explosion of new breweries and brewpubs that has occurred over the last few years.

Despite the statistical fact that Texas ranks poorly for breweries per capita—forty-second out of fifty-one states in 2012, according to the Brewers Association—I'd stated a couple of years ago that the Austin craft beer scene was saturated and couldn't support more due to the unfamiliarity of beer styles to Austin consumers.

I'm glad to admit that I was wrong, as more breweries in production are announced at a staggering rate. It is also a good reminder of what sets Austin apart from other beer-centric cities. Austin brewers offer a diverse portfolio of craft beers to satisfy every palate. While brewers along the Pacific Coast are pressured to create the next greatest West Coast IPA, Austin breweries are introducing beer styles that have previously been considered inaccessible, including Austin Beer Works's Einhorn Berliner weissbier, Hops & Grain's Alt-eration, Rogness Brewing's Beardy Guard, as well as many others.

While in Austin for his performance at the Austin City Limits Festival (ACL), where I transported musical artists to and from the site, banjo player Béla Fleck asked, "Debbie, tell me what it is you like about Austin—and don't say it's the music."

It only took a few seconds to answer, "The sense of community." Whether it's charity, music, film or beer, Austin is made up of people who come together to share their passion. The Austin beer community is a shining example, with craft beer enthusiasts and bloggers supporting the breweries and brewpubs and brewers helping one another with ingredients and equipment, as well as mutual support to the local homebrew community.

Nowhere else in the nation could a cooperative brewpub such as Black Star Co-op have taken root and flourished during an unstable economic landscape, not to mention inspired people to open a similar model in their own city.

Be prepared to learn more in *Austin Beer* about this unique concept as well as key personalities who have made the Austin beer scene what it is today. Among those who make an appearance are brewers such as Tim Schwartz, who was the first local pro to make a commercially available beer out of rainwater in 2004; Brian Peters, who after years of supporting others has opened his own brewpub, ABGB; and Steve Anderson, who has also been instrumental in multiple craft beer–related establishments and now owns a brewery in Alpine, Texas. And there are many, many more!

Debbie Cerda
Austin Zealots
Founder of Austin Women's Beer League
American Homebrewers' Association Governing Committee

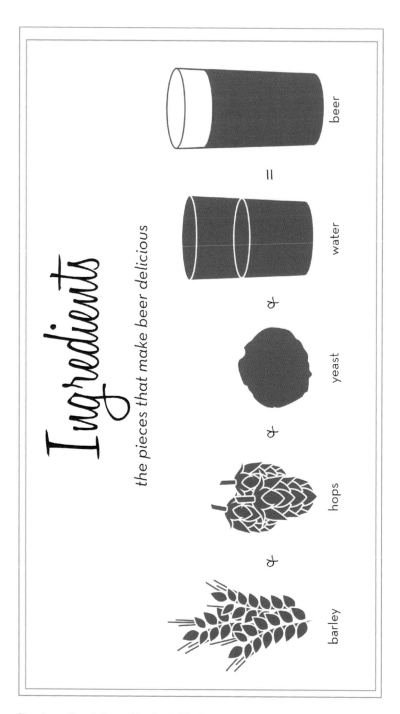

Beer ingredient infographic. *Sarah Wood*.

INTRODUCTION

Austin, Texas, has long been dubbed the "Live Music Capital of the World." Now, Bob Schneider and Shakey Graves are great and all, but what you should really come here for is the beer. Name a style, and you can probably find a brewery that makes it. Whether you're an IPA drinker or love a good Belgian (don't we all?) there is a wide breadth of choices and a deep history of brewing to explore while you're here.

Over the last few decades, Austin has seen abundant growth in its beer industry. In 2012 alone, five breweries burst onto the already booming beer scene. From Pflugerville to Blanco, Central Texas is teeming with innovative and passionate brewers who have brought a previously one-beer town into a time of distinctly Austin brews.

The beer scene in Austin predates Prohibition: one of the city's first commercial brewer's vaults, built in the early 1860s, now lies under a Mexican restaurant in the heart of downtown. Don't let that depress you, though. La Condesa has repurposed the vaults and now uses them to serve trendy Austin crowds delicious tostadas.

Post-Prohibition has proven to be a much more fruitful time in Austin's beer history. The town is now rich with breweries, brewpubs (yes, we make that distinction in Texas) and craft beer bars. Slowly but surely, craft beer is taking over Austin. Though it has yet to break into the big party district of Sixth Street proper, most other parts of town have their own neighborhood dive where you can stop in for a pint of local craft beer.

If you prefer to brew your own beer, Austin Homebrew Supply is your mecca. Its binder full of recipes and shelves full of yeast strains are enough to make any avid homebrewer drool. The bearded men behind the counter have a wealth of knowledge and are eager to help you start your next badass batch of homemade beer. In true Texas tradition, most of our brewers started by making beer at home. A few of them even started when they could only legally buy the malt and hops but not the beer itself. From backyard brewing to Austin Zealots Homebrew Club meetings, Austin thoroughly embraces this avenue of craft beer expression.

In what can only be referred to as a second wind, Austin has seen growth from a few large breweries to a brewery to fit every style and taste. The '90s saw the expansion of breweries across Central Texas, and the breweries that appeared during that time made local beer more prevalent on tap walls and store shelves. Through the building of this great "brewmunity," all breweries can be represented on the same cooler shelf.

Austin's craft beer community is marked by its support for its members, which creates a general feeling of solidarity. While they may be in competition on local tap walls, Austin breweries will still gladly lend a bag of grain to a friend in need. The Texas beer community sticks together, and the ties that bind it are strong. For *Bitch Beer*, becoming a part of this community has been an excellent adventure thus far.

In this growing beer-conomy we, the lady-bloggers at BitchBeer.Org, chose to use our free time to write about Austin beer because we discovered actually drinking beer is only half the fun. *Bitch Beer* started in the beautiful taproom of Thirsty Planet Brewing Company, a brewery just south of Austin. Looking around, we noticed that we were the only unattached females there. After one boozy afternoon at Thirsty Planet, we were sold on the idea of starting a woman-run blog about beer. We immediately bought a URL and started writing. From that point on, we have covered features, events and general beer news and have loved every minute of it.

You may ask, why the name *Bitch Beer*? Well, we're glad you did. Bitch beer is a colloquialism for those sickeningly sweet malt beverages that were a necessary add-on for frat parties so that the girls "would have something to drink." At *Bitch Beer*, we are reclaiming that term and flipping it on its head. We love to drink quality craft beer, so we are out to prove that if bitch beer is beer for girls, then every beer is bitch beer. Women, just like their male counterparts, drink everything from hefeweizens to stouts, and we are damn proud of it.

In this book, we hope to give you our take on Texas craft beer along with its history—past, present and future. This book is the culmination of more than

Austin Beer writers (from left to right) Kat McCullough, Arianna Auber, Holly Aker, Wendy Cawthon, Shaun Martin, Sarah Wood and Caroline Wallace.

sixty interviews with members of the Austin brewing community. This is their story as much as ours, and we are honored to share it. We highly recommend grabbing a beer now, as this book might cause the urge to drink a good craft brew.

Cheers!
From the Capital City

Drinking Game

As you read this book, we suggest you always have a beer in hand. Follow along with the drinking game and local beer pairings in each chapter for an engaging reading experience. After all, you're never (drinking) alone when in the company of a good book.

Drink when you find:

1. A thinly veiled innuendo.
2. A beer-related, made-up word (BREWmunity, BREWconomy, etc.).
3. A hashtag.
4. A photo of a bearded man.
5. An approximate date used in lieu of a specific one (these interviewees have a torrid and boozy past, people).
6. A brewery that has named a beer after a dog, historical figure or Austin landmark.
7. A reference to someone moving to Austin.
8. "Swifty."
9. A photo of beer being poured.

(Diminish the future resale value of this book by writing in your own rules below.)

10. _____

11. _____

And of course, drink whenever you get thirsty.

CHAPTER ONE
OLD SCHOOL BREWS: AUSTIN'S FIRST BREWERIES

PAIRS WITH LIVE OAK HEFEWEIZEN

Like so many riddles of our historical past, scattered accounts of Austin's early brewing traditions have narrowly survived to present day. Much of what we know about beer production in the eighty-odd years between Austin's settlement and the onslaught of Prohibition comes cloaked in the obscurity of vague historical documents, faded newspaper clippings and retold oral histories. It seems that in many cases, the stories, recipes and practices of Austin's earliest breweries might have simply gone down the drain.

While today college students, musicians, government workers and creative types populate the capital city, the first people to pass through this part of the Texas Hill Country belonged to the Comanche, Tonkawa and Lipan Apache Indian tribes. It wasn't until hundreds of years later, in the 1830s, that European settlers began to arrive in the area and erect permanent structures. "Waterloo," as they soon christened their new frontier outpost, sat on the north bank of the Colorado River, near where the Congress Avenue Bridge begins today. Less than a decade after it was settled, Waterloo was declared the capital of the newly sovereign Republic of Texas, and the small town began to experience rapid growth. Waterloo was soon renamed Austin, to honor Stephen F. Austin, also known as the "Father of Texas." By 1840, the city had ballooned to 850 occupants. With a now-burgeoning population, people began to ask, "Where can an early settler get a beer around here?"

JOHANN "JEAN" SCHNEIDER

Johann "Jean" Schneider was one of Austin's first commercial brewers. Schneider, a German immigrant who carried his brewing knowledge across the Atlantic, first arrived in Central Texas sometime between 1845 and 1846. He made his home in the Fisher-Miller Colony, a German settlement located about forty-five miles south of Austin, near modern-day New Braunfels. By the late 1850s, the Schneider family did what so many Californians who visit for South by Southwest (SXSW) do today: they decided to move to Austin.

On April 14, 1860, Schneider took out an advertisement in the *State Gazette* to announce the grand opening of his brewery, which he was operating out of the back of Kirchberg's Saloon on Congress Avenue. From this early brewpub of sorts, Schneider brewed traditional German lagers, a trade he learned by working for several years in the most "extensive and renowned breweries in Europe," at least according to his own words in the advertisement.

Schneider advertised his beers as being free from narcotics and other "unwholesome" ingredients. This fact, combined with his German heritage, suggests that Schneider brewed his lagers in accordance to *Reinheitsgebot*, also known as "German Purity Law." The decree, first set forward in Germany in 1487, ordained that beer could only be composed of three basic ingredients—water, hops and barley. Obviously, there is one sort of essential ingredient missing here—yeast. At the time, beer was regularly brewed in open vessels, and sediment from previous batches was often passed on to the next batch. However, it was not until 1857 that French scientist Louis Pasteur discovered that yeast, a living microorganism, plays the key role in the fermentation of alcoholic beverages.

Surprisingly, only three short years after Pasteur's discovery, a continent away, in an era in which news didn't exactly travel fast (#SnailMail), there is actually evidence that Schneider was not only actively inoculating his beers with yeast but that he understood the dual function of yeast for both brewing and baking. In addition to selling his beer out of Kirchberg's, Schneider would also sell fresh yeast to local bread makers, promising that after they tried baking with his yeast, they would never go back to using other leavening agents, such as baking soda, again.

Schneider's claims about his beer's cleanliness were not just ye olde advertising puffery. During this same time period in Europe, some brewers were actively mixing narcotics—such as *Cocculus indicus*, which contained a poisonous alkaloid with stimulant properties—into their beer because it bolstered the beer's intoxicating effects. Think of it as a nineteenth century version of the Irish car bomb, except even more toxic. Even in the much

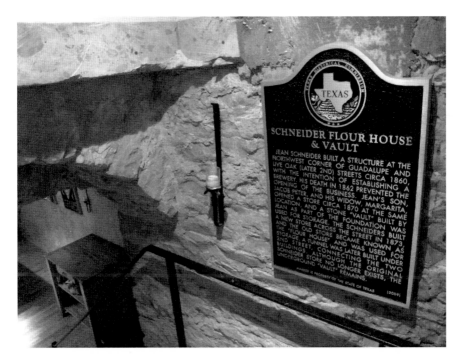

Schneider's beer vaults were declared a Texas State Historical Site in 2009. *Caroline Wallace.*

earlier years of the century, between 1813 and 1819, at least fifty brewers and retailers back in Germany were tried and convicted for adding ingredients to beer. Some of these ingredients were as benign as ginger or coriander seeds, but a large percentage of those convicted were using cocculus. Any substance used for alcohol boosting or to encourage intoxicating or hallucinogenic effects would have been highly frowned upon in Austin during this time period. Even in 1860, pleas for temperance were permeating, and it was important for lager beer to be considered exempt due to its lower alcohol content. Because session beers are practically as innocuous as water, right?

The Schneider family made their home a few blocks away from Kirchberg's, off Guadalupe and Live Oak (now known as Second Street). It was below this family homestead that Schneider built two limestone beer vaults to store his beer. Before the rise of refrigeration, it was not possible to brew or store lager at proper temperatures during the warmer months of the year without the aid of some kind of cool, often subterranean environment. These vaults, which had high ceilings and low archways, were the first of their kind in Austin and were the beginning of a new, larger brewery for

Schneider. However, it is unlikely that Schneider ever actually got the chance to use these vaults for brewing. After a brief enlistment in the Confederate army, Schneider died January 18, 1862, in a wagon accident. Schneider's beer vaults were discovered in 2000 during a large-scale construction project in the Second Street District. After being deemed significant by the Texas Historical Commission, the German brewer's vaults are now preserved (with a historical plaque and everything) and used as a private subterranean dining room for the trendy modern Mexican restaurant La Condesa.

CITY BREWERY

An 1877 map of Austin produced by the Sanborn Fire Insurance Agency reveals perhaps the only known diagram of a brewery operating at 300 Guadalupe Street on the corner of Live Oak (Second Street). The brewery stood mere blocks from where Jean Schneider had planned to build his brewery in the previous decade. The establishment was rather imaginatively named "City Brewery," and the brewmaster of the new operation was a Prussian-born cabinetmaker named Frederick W. Sutor.

According to a relative's later recounting, Sutor married his wife, Emily, in Prussia sometime in the early 1850s, and the newlyweds immediately set sail for America, spending their honeymoon at sea. As has been the case with pretty much every story of crossing the Atlantic, inconsistent winds caused for a lengthier, more treacherous journey than originally anticipated, but just as their supply of canned food started to wane, they made port in Houston. (It just might have been the only time in recorded history that people were actually happy to arrive in Houston.) However, once there, they had the good sense to load up their wagons and make their way to Austin. Once they arrived, the Sutors built a log cabin near where Congress Avenue hits the Colorado River. They had a rash of bad luck in the housing department, as that first house was swept away by floodwaters from the river. They sought higher ground, building a new home on the west side of Congress Avenue between Third and Fourth Streets. A fire damaged that house a few years later, but neighbors joined forces to help the Sutors rebuild. In addition to crafting cabinets, Sutor worked as a saddle maker for some time before opening a general store with a man named Henry Hirshfeld from 1856 to 1859.

Little is known about Sutor's motives for starting a brewery, besides, of course, the fact that breweries are magical places that happen to contain

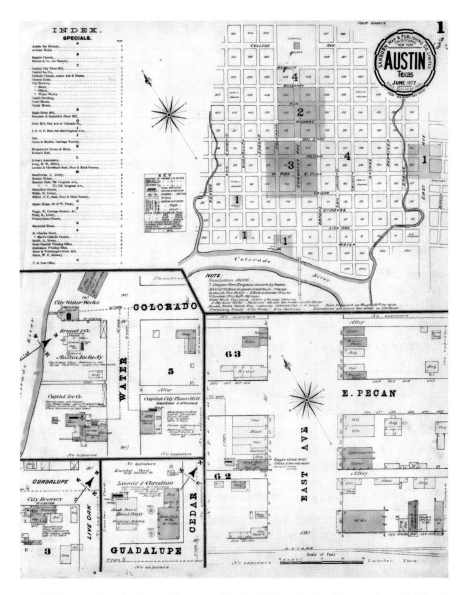

An 1877 map of Austin shows a diagram of Frederick Sutor's City Brewery (lower left-hand corner). *Perry-Castañeda Library Map Collection, University of Texas at Austin Libraries.*

beer. Or, maybe it was the fact that Sutor actually had ten kids at home, which could probably drive anyone to drink. There isn't any evidence of Sutor brewing back in Prussia or in his early days in Austin, but nevertheless, he began crafting German-style lagers at the City Brewery in 1874. Of the brewery's features outlined on the 1877 Sanborn map, two kettles, a mash tun and a room for empty keg storage are visible.

Sutor did try to sell the brewery in a newspaper ad in 1875, but it appears he never went through with a sale and continued to brew up until his death in 1878 at the age of fifty-nine. It is unclear whether the brewery continued to operate after his death, but the *Mooney & Morrison's General Directory for 1877–78* lists another man, Anton Gruber, as a brewer at City Brewery. Whether Gruber worked under Sutor or took over the brewery after his death is also unknown, but the next Sanborn map made of downtown in 1885 shows Calcasieu Lumber Co. occupying the former City Brewery building. The same series of general directories tells us that by 1885, Gruber was working as the beer wagon driver for Anheuser-Busch. By 1889, he was driving beer for Lone Star Brewing Company.

Emily Sutor outlived her husband by nearly forty years, going on to own properties around town and rent out a series of cabins for income. She was said to be a good manager and frugal businesswoman.

PRESSLER'S BEER GARDEN

Paul Pressler was yet another German immigrant to play a key role in crafting Austin's brewing industry. Born in Torgau, Germany, in 1835, Torgau would later become known as the town where U.S. and Soviet forces met during World War II. (Also, the town is home to a castle with a moat full of bears; google it.) After immigrating to Austin, Pressler started brewing beer with his brothers Frank and Ernest on some family land up on Manor Road, which was about three miles northeast of town at the time. Their uncle Charles Pressler was a well-known Texas mapmaker and responsible for funding the endeavor. The brothers brewed there from 1860 to 1862 until all three joined the Confederate army. A while after returning from the war, in 1874, Pressler started brewing again, this time, at 1327 West Sixth Street.

Pressler referred to his brewery as a "Steam Brewery." The steam beer style is now synonymous with San Francisco–based Anchor Brewing's flagship, Anchor Steam. So synonymous, in fact, that as the only brewery to continue brewing steam beer after the repeal of Prohibition, they actually copyrighted the term. Other breweries that now brew the same style refer to it as California common. But long before that, far from the Golden State, Pressler was brewing something he called steam beer in Austin. Steam beers

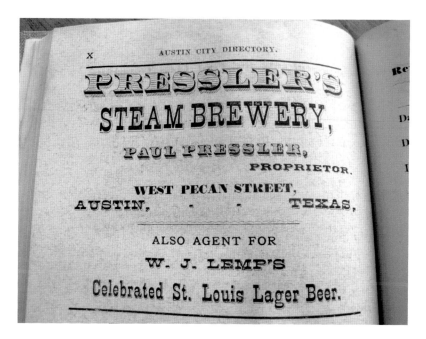

Paul Pressler advertised his brewery as a Steam Brewery. It remains unclear whether the brewery brewed traditional steam beer or was fueled by a steam engine. *From* Mooney & Morrison's General Directory of the City of Austin, Texas, for 1877–78.

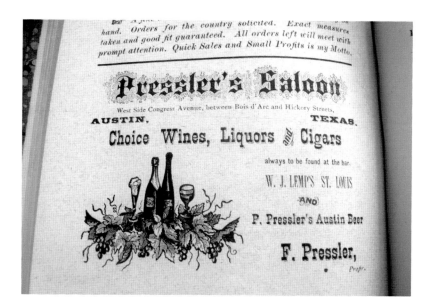

An 1877 advertisement for Frank Pressler's Congress Avenue saloon. *From* Mooney & Morrison's General Directory of the City of Austin, Texas, for 1877–78.

are essentially lagers fermented at the warmer temperatures traditionally reserved for ales. It was a style that arose out of equal parts ingenuity and desperation, as temperatures, and even water, in the American West were typically too warm in the summer months for lagers to ferment at the appropriate low temperature. But with no ties to the western United States, it is unlikely that Pressler began brewing steam beer to emulate Californians. What is more likely is that, being German, he called his beer steam beer because he brewed the same traditional German beer style Dampfbier (aka the original California common), which literally translates to steam beer. Or, perhaps his brewery was actually powered by a steam engine. Unfortunately, the answer may be lost to history.

Eventually, Pressler's brother Frank—who owned a saloon on Congress Avenue at the time—joined forces to create Pressler's Beer Garden (although an advertisement in the 1877 Austin city directory suggests that Frank continued to operate Pressler's Saloon as well and even served his brother's beer there, too). Beginning on the corner of Sixth Street, which was then called Pecan Street, and what is now, appropriately, named Pressler Street, this massive "Austin Pleasure Resort" stretched almost half a mile, all the way to the river. Old advertisements for the place read more as though they were touting a country club than a brewery, though with its expansive estate and myriad activities, it might as well have been. Besides enjoying freshly brewed draught beer, patrons also had access to the grounds, which housed a fountain, croquet course, dance pavilion, swings, games, a boating house, bandstand, a Schützenverein—better known here as a gun club—and even an alligator pond.

While the combination of intoxication, firearms and man-eating reptiles might not exactly sound like the safest way to spend a Saturday night, Pressler's, like the other beer gardens in those days, prided itself on being a respectable family establishment, far from the debauchery of the saloons and brothels found in Austin's then-emerging downtown red-light district dubbed "Guy Town." Pressler's was so set on carving out a respectable reputation that one 1887 advertisement promised that "dancing, swinging, croqueting and games of various kinds may be indulged in with perfect quiet and safety from the intrusion of rough or improper characters." Far from these intrusions it was. Even though Pressler's was located only around a mile from downtown, the barren road leading to it was pure country. In fact, in an undated account titled *O. Henry's Wedding*, Lawrence K. Smoot looked back on Pressler's glory days, saying "Pecan Street, though called a street, was just a lonesome, dusty, country road, and a plodding horse could raise more dust in twenty feet than an automobile does in a mile." Perhaps ironically, it was

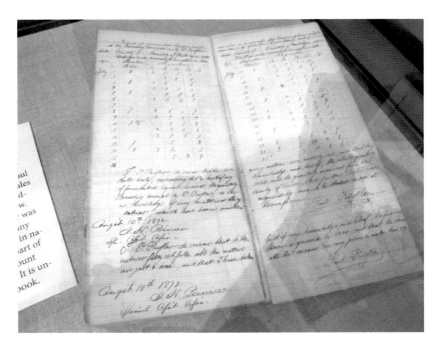

Paul Pressler's brewing ledger is on display at the Austin History Center. *Caroline Wallace.*

Refrigerated train cars allowed large breweries to transport fresh beer farther than ever before. *C.G.P. Grey.*

Pressler's idyllic, pastoral location that eventually served as the catalyst to its demise. After around thirty years in business, the city expanded westward, and Pressler's was gobbled up by residential development. (That residential shift has persisted. Today, a luxury apartment complex occupies a portion of the former Pressler's grounds.) It's believed that brewing operations at Pressler's actually stopped there much earlier than the beer garden's closure, by one account as early as 1878, due to competition from larger, out-of-town breweries with flashy advertising and superior industrial technology. Whether it was true or not (hard to do a taste test now), conventional consumer wisdom at the time was that these larger breweries were not only selling beer at comparable prices but were also producing a superior product.

Long before Pressler's Beer Garden actually shuttered, Paul Pressler began moonlighting for W.M.J. Lemp Brewing Company, one of the companies that would eventually cause local beer production in Austin to evaporate. Pressler served as the local Austin agent for the large St. Louis–based brewery that rose to national prominence with the advent of refrigerated train cars. Lemp Brewing was an industrial marvel of its time. Hell, many microbreweries today would still be jealous of its output capabilities. By 1894, Lemp was reportedly putting out 300,000 barrels a year, and their bottling line could accommodate 100,000 bottles in a single day. The company had seven hundred employees, a team of one hundred horses and four hundred refrigerated train cars to facilitate deliveries across the country. Pressler's Lemp office in Austin was located on Cypress Street (Third Street) between Guadalupe and San Antonio and housed ice-filled cellars large enough to contain three carloads of beer. Paul Pressler continued to serve as the Lemp agent until his death in 1894, when his son August Pressler succeeded him in the position.

Lemp Brewing is just one example of a large national brewery that was able to take advantage of new technologies, such as refrigeration and mechanized bottling lines, to put out higher quantities of beer and ship them fresh to farther corners of the United States than previously thought possible. As early as 1885, St. Louis–based Anheuser-Busch and San Antonio–based breweries Belohradsky J.B. & Co. and Lone Star Brewing Company all had distribution offices in Austin. In fact, under the directory heading "Breweries" in *Morrison & Fourmy's General Directory of the City of Austin, 1885–1886*, there are no actual local brewing facilities listed, only distributors' storage and sales facilities. It seems that at least for a time, the Austin brewing industry had fallen prey to the appeal of national brands.

CHAPTER TWO

PROHIBITION:
THE ULTIMATE BUZZ KILL

PAIRS WITH JESTER KING LE PETIT PRINCE

In 1919, the federal government passed the Eighteenth Amendment, placing a nationwide ban on all alcoholic beverages that went into effect on January 17, 1920. It remained law for thirteen agonizing, beerless years, and Austin was not spared. Texas had around forty-three breweries from 1890 to 1918. Many of them closed for a variety of reasons such as lack of capital, inferior products or an inability to compete with larger breweries. However, some closed due to measures that allowed cities and towns to declare themselves dry. Eventually, once the national Prohibition came into effect, the final thirteen breweries in the only wet counties closed their doors for good. But as the saying goes, you gotta fight for your right to party. The fight against Prohibition, however, raged long before the Eighteenth Amendment and the Volstead Act were passed.

PROHIBITION HITS TEXAS

When people first started moving to Texas, it is assumed that the colonists brought the burgeoning temperance movement with them. Temperance is the idea that people should abstain from drinking of their own volition, whereas Prohibition is a national ban on all alcohol. Both were just whispers in the country, starting with the first temperance society in 1789. However, these beliefs faded somewhat in the harsh pioneer country of the early Republic of Texas, which is understandable when you're building log cabins and other structures literally from scratch. Early colonists also might not have known where safe water was at the time, and oftentimes, as we all know, beer has historically been a safer (and tastier) alternative.

Movement toward Prohibition resurfaced when the first liquor law in Texas—a tax on wet goods in 1837—was passed by the congress of the republic. It placed a tax on taverns and saloons along with a tax on wine and spirits. For whatever reason, beer and cider were spared from the tax. It could have been due to water conditions in the early days in Texas, or beer's lower alcohol content or, maybe, the congressmen just had a soft spot for beer (i.e. a raging dependency). Either way, beer was untaxed for three years, until the Republic of Texas amended tax laws to include ciders and malt liquors.

The anti-alcohol faction began to bolster increased support in Texas around this time, and it mainly sought to educate people about temperance instead of outlawing all alcoholic beverages. Prohibitionists believed that alcohol would crumble society and was a huge factor contributing toward crime and poverty. The struggle between the Drys (those for Prohibition) and the Wets (those against Prohibition) in Texas began in the 1840s when the Drys sought to add measures that would allow voters the option of declaring their neighborhoods, towns, cities and counties dry.

Eventually, the Drys, figuratively drunk on their own power, would demand statewide Prohibition along with an amendment to the constitution to make it law. Texas began the move toward Prohibition early on with some small amendments to the state constitution and some harsh laws on alcohol. In 1845, a law that banned saloons in Texas was passed—however, this law was never really enforced. This did not stop the movement, as it began to pick up steam. The first legislation for Texas liquor control was proposed on August 7, 1854. The law sought to ban "dram-shops" which sold liquor in quantities less than one quart. The court case of *State v. Swisher* was brought up before a Hays County court and attacked the constitutionality of this law. Before the case was even determined, the Texas government quickly repealed the law, which led some to believe that the author knew the law was unconstitutional.

Texas continued to add more regulatory laws and amendments to the state constitution over the next twenty years. In 1861, a tax was placed on breweries and businesses selling beer. Interestingly enough, this law was the first to use the word "brewery" and was the first occupation tax on everyone manufacturing or selling beer. During the state's eleventh legislature, the congress approved an amendment to a law passed in 1856 that placed conditions on obtaining a license to run the 1800s equivalent of a bar. A few of the conditions included keeping an orderly house, closing house on Sundays and not selling alcohol to minors under sixteen—oh, the good ol' days when sixteen-year-olds were legally allowed to drink.

In 1876, Texas would add a provision for local-option elections into its constitution. On December 18 of that year, Jasper County was the first county to vote dry. Harry Haynes, a member of the Friends of Temperance, worked with Judge Simkins, a member of the legislature of 1887, to amend the local-option law to make it more attractive and worthwhile to adopt, much like how some definitely non-craft big name beer companies will try to play off their beer as "craft" to garner more appeal. In the next few years, the local-option law would spread, taking North, East and West Texas with it (#Sheeple).

The first vote for a statewide Prohibition amendment occurred during an election on August 4, 1887, and was defeated by a vote of 220,627 to 129,270. Many considered this defeat to be the "Waterloo of Prohibition in Texas." However, in the following years, many counties adopted the local-option law. It is speculated that this was spurred on by discussion regarding the civic righteousness of Prohibition leading up to the 1887 election.

MAJOR PLAYERS INVOLVED IN TEXAS PROHIBITION

Major parties in the Prohibition controversy began to hit the scene in 1870 with the United Friends of Temperance becoming the first Texas-wide dry organization. It was a secret fraternity of sorts, which demanded its members pledge total abstinence from liquor. The organization helped alcoholics return from their addiction to drink, educated the young on the dangers of alcohol and strived to turn public sentiment against liquor. The Friends of Temperance even had a youth organization called "Bands of Hope," which consisted of boys and girls promising abstinence from alcohol, tobacco and profanity (and fun, apparently).

Dr. James Younge was the foundation on which the organization was built. Younge went around Texas, lecturing on the dangers of alcohol, and eventually ended up moving to Texas. Younge formed an estimated 1,500 Temperance Councils and 800 Bands of Hope groups in the state. Unfortunately for the Friends of Temperance, the election in 1887 was a killing blow for the organization. Since the Friends of Temperance failed to create a statewide prohibition on alcohol, the group broke apart and focused its efforts on taking the state county by county.

Another group involved in Texas's temperance movement was the Woman's Christian Temperance Union. The union's Texas branch (TWCTU) was founded in 1883 after the national WCTU's president, Frances E. Willard, wrote to a minister in Paris, Texas, saying that she would like to come down to organize Texas's women against the power of the liquor distributors. The minister did not want to be responsible in case the organization failed because, according to records, there was a strong dislike of women in the Prohibition platform in the early days. So he gave the letter to Colonel Ebeneezer Lafayette Dohoney, believed to be the Father of Prohibition, who was ecstatic about getting Willard down to Texas. However, the dislike for women taking a political role in Prohibition was so strong that no church in Texas would let Willard organize in its facilities. Dohoney had to rent an opera house for Willard to preach in. A huge crowd of women came to listen to Willard, and on May 9, 1882, the first TWCTU was formed in Colonel Dohoney's parlor. Willard went on to create unions in Austin, Waco, San Antonio and Houston, among other locations.

The purpose of the WCTU was to promote total abstinence from alcoholic beverages in an effort to prevent crime and immorality. Women were also big fans of Prohibition due to the fact that alcohol could make an abusive husband pretty much Hulk out. Spousal abuse also wasn't formally recognized as a crime during those days. So yeah, women had beef with alcohol at the time. The organization ended up being used to promote the possibility of women in a public and political role—something we can get behind as long as they keep temperance out of the equation. Lala Fay Watts was the Austin TWCTU chapter's president and committed herself to the TWCTU's cause. At the helm of the organization, Watts used the union to lobby for stricter enforcement of Prohibition laws and for electing dry candidates to different levels of office. She would remain the president of the union chapter for nearly forty years before going on to campaign for women's suffrage.

A vast majority of Texas women were in total support of Prohibition. When Prohibitionists began to take notice of this large group, significant numbers of men started to fight for women's suffrage. On the other end of

Political cartoon satirizes WCTU and its agenda. Hawaiian Gazette, *May 23, 1902.*
University of Hawaii at Manoa Library.

the spectrum, those in the brewing and liquor industry were not incredibly supportive of women's suffrage. When you have a large group trying to undermine your business, you kind of want to undermine its freedoms (#AmIRight?). Brewers spent a considerable amount of time fighting against the suffrage movement. (It should go without saying that an antiwoman sentiment is thankfully nonexistent for brewers in Austin today.)

As with many large-scale social movements, a political party rose from the debate. The Prohibition Party was first introduced into Texas by none other than Colonel Dohoney. The man liked his Prohibition and, with a name like "Ebeneezer," he was destined to be a killer of joy—a scrooge, if you will. The first convention of Prohibitionists was held on September 8, 1884, in Fort Worth. Leading up to the election of 1887, the Prohibition Party held the first state Prohibition Party convention in September 1886. They adopted a platform that demanded submission to Prohibition and nominated none other than E.L. Dohoney for governor and Dr. F.E. Yoakum for lieutenant governor.

By 1895, 79 of the 239 counties in Texas were partly dry and 53 were completely dry. Most of them were rural counties, while the more urban areas and cities along the border between Texas and Mexico refused to let go of their alcohol.

Working with the United Friends of Temperance, WCTU and the Prohibition Party, the Anti-Saloon League began a national crusade against alcoholic beverages in 1913, when they began to draft an amendment that would demand national Prohibition. U.S. senator Morris Sheppard of Texas helped to push for the bill's passage. Sheppard was deeply progressive and truly felt that alcohol was a serious danger to the nation. Prohibition was always at the top of his list of reforms, and Sheppard also forsook coffee, tea and tobacco. Sheppard worked closely with the Anti-Saloon League and the WCTU to push for stricter Prohibition laws. He also slept sixteen hours a day, and none of the other senators thought he was cool.

Many spoke out against the amendment that the Anti-Saloon League was trying to pass, including former Texas governor Joseph Bailey. He considered the measure a dangerous precedent and thought making the amendment a national solution to a social problem would cause other reformers to go the same route. Of course, with his defense of alcohol, Bailey went on to add that the country would see national women's suffrage and national divorce and marriage laws, as well as interracial marriages—as though those were bad things.

Austin experienced its own clash of the Drys versus the Wets. These two parties had a long tug of war over Austin's wet nature. Prohibitionists tried and failed in the 1908 and 1911 elections to turn Austin into a dry city. Despite these failures, the number of dry counties in Texas was increasing, and Austin soon joined their ranks. Once the Eighteenth Amendment passed in 1918, it took only a year before Texas would approve a state Prohibition amendment, HJR 1, which prohibited anyone in Texas from the manufacture, sale, barter or exchange of alcohol, passed with 159,723 votes for and 140,099 votes against on May 24, 1919.

Once the amendment was added, the Anti-Saloon League became divided over how to approach it. Members could not decide if they wanted to play good cop or bad cap: treat the amendment as a way of persuading Americans to abstain from liquor or as a way to demand strict enforcement. At the time, opponents of Prohibition controlled the Texas government and refused to enforce the laws.

Border control officers confiscate liquor in Marfa during Prohibition. *Marfa Public Library, Portal to Texas History.*

The state leader of the Anti-Saloon League of Texas, Atticus Webb, failed miserably to obtain a strict enforcement approach to the amendment. Webb went somewhat overboard when it came to Prohibition and enforcing the law. News articles from the time claimed that Webb demanded an investigation of a celebratory barbecue in Amarillo because the hosts were allegedly serving alcohol to their guests. Apparently, there was a tin bucket of liquor at a ranch house near the barbecue. Once the scandal came to light at the party and people started noticing that a lot of the guests were drunk, they did what any high schoolers throwing a party when their parents are out of town do: they destroyed the evidence.

This was not the only example of Webb's love affair with the Eighteenth Amendment. In 1927, Webb began a nationwide tour to explain the good that Prohibition had done for the country and shame the propagandists claiming that it was a failure. Webb presented facts and statistics from various sources in what was called the "Unfinished Task." He claimed that there was a 90 percent decrease in drinking, which resulted in an annual decrease in drunkenness by about 500,000 cases. There was also a decrease in crime, and he claimed that church membership had risen by about 5,317,000 people.

The Final Countdown for Prohibition

Some businesses found ways to cope with the sudden passing of Prohibition. Scholz Garten, a local Austin beer garden, opened in 1866 after August Scholz purchased an old building that had served as a boardinghouse from Sam Norville for $2,400 a few years earlier. Over time, Scholz added the Biergarten and Scholz's popularity increased. Scholz became a popular spot for the German population to meet and enjoy German-style food. He died in 1891, and his son sold the tavern to Lemp Brewing Company. Then in 1908, a German singing group, the Austin Saengerrunde, purchased the tavern. Scholz Garten managed to stay afloat by moving its attention to the sale of food. Food sales at Scholz Garten increased by 50 percent and continue to be its biggest seller. Further undaunted by Prohibition, Scholz created a nonalcoholic beer in 1921, aptly naming it the "Bone Dry Beer," which became a hit with patrons.

Other companies that stayed afloat in the wake of Prohibition included the Galveston Brewing Company. The brewery was shut down in 1916 in anticipation of Prohibition. In 1895, the company changed its name to Southern Beverage Company and began selling soft drinks that consisted mainly of ginger ale and root beer under the brand name XXX. It became increasingly popular when Southern Beverage Company set up "Thirst Stations," or drive-ins, for root beer. Triple XXX operated a Thirst Station in Austin right on Guadalupe Street. The Thirst Stations were an attempt to ease the pain of the Eighteenth Amendment's passing. Think of it as your favorite bar, only not as boozy. To this day, Triple XXX has stuck to the root beer that kept them afloat during Prohibition.

In the end, Prohibition's support began to waver in the wake of the Great Depression, which began in 1929. By 1933, the Eighteenth Amendment was repealed through the passage of the Twenty-first Amendment, the first and only amendment to the United States Constitution to render a previous one moot. That same year, during Texas's forty-third legislature, Texans voted for the Twenty-first Amendment, but it had no effect due to the 1919 state Prohibition amendment. However, during this same vote, Texans voted in favor of a bill that would allow beer with a 3.2 percent ABV to be sold. Within a few months, this lower alcohol beer began selling. In 1935, Texan voters repealed the state dry law, and the law returned to the local level. Photographs from this time period showed what were known as Falstaff beer trucks, owned by Lemp Brewing Company (the same company that bought Scholz Garten and earlier employed Paul Pressler), parked outside

Scholz Garten survived Prohibition and is still a popular watering hole today. *Larry D. Moore.*

the capitol building and their drivers standing at the ready to deliver beer to thirsty Austinites.

As you can imagine, once Prohibition was repealed, businesses across the country wanted to get their hands on a liquor license. John Kenneth Threadgill, who moved to Austin in 1933, started working at an old service station on North Lamar Boulevard. By the end of the year, he bought the service station and converted it to Threadgill's Tavern. After Prohibition was repealed, Threadgill's Tavern was the first business in Austin to operate under a beer license. The reactions to Threadgill's beer license after thirteen years of Prohibition were probably similar to every South by Southwest attendee's reaction to parties that offer free beer and food.

Prohibition's impact lingered in the state of Texas until 1970, when Texans voted to remove the ban on "open saloons." They approved the sale of mixed alcoholic beverages, or liquor by the drink, on a local-option basis. Unfortunately, the impact of Prohibition in Austin is still in the air. There are still certain blue laws (laws created to enforce religious standards) that were passed during Prohibition. One such blue law involves banning the sale of liquor by the bottle on Sundays. The option-only law still remains in effect, and there are a number of dry counties in the state of Texas to this day—Austin is, thankfully, not one of them.

CHAPTER THREE
AUSTIN'S CRAFT BEER RENAISSANCE

PAIRS WITH REAL ALE HANS PILS

The 1990s were a pivotal time in Austin's craft beer history, during which current local staples, such as Live Oak Brewing and Real Ale Brewing Co., opened and sparked a veritable renaissance of craft beer. Sales of craft beer rose at this time, and many grocery stores began to actively stock craft beers to cash in on the sudden interest they received.

CELIS BREWING

While most kids spend their childhood years swinging from monkey bars and climbing up jungle gyms, Christine Celis's playscape of choice was a little different. Daughter of famed brewmaster Pierre Celis, she spent her formative years frolicking around his brewery in Hoegaarden, Belgium. Her connection to the art of brewing at such an early age was fitting, because Pierre learned to brew beer when he was not much more than a child himself.

In that same village of Hoegaarden, at the tender age of sixteen, Pierre started to learn the craft of making traditional Belgian witbier. This was the 1940s, but the cloudy, unfiltered wheat beer had been brewed in Hoegaarden since the Middle Ages. His teacher, a neighbor named Louis Tomsin, brewed the witbier for the village at the time. With no children of his own, Tomsin treated Pierre like the son he never had. He eventually took him on as his apprentice of sorts and let him help out in the brewery, teaching him the centuries-old craft along the way. When Tomsin passed away in the late 1950s, it seemed as if he had effectively taken the Belgian witbier with him to his grave, as it was not brewed again for nearly a decade. But all that changed one night in 1966, when Pierre got a little good old-fashioned peer pressure from friends at a local pub. Longing for the thirst-quenching beer they had such fond memories of, they wondered if Pierre might still recall the recipe. To their surprise, Pierre told them he actually still had a few of Tomsin's old bottles tucked away at home. After breaking into some of the beer, his friends grew even more nostalgic, realizing how much they truly missed that taste. However, they would soon learn that the beer they were enjoying so much was no relic from a bygone era at all, but rather a new batch of homebrew Pierre had been tinkering around with to see if he could still master the old recipe. Excited that his homage had passed for the real deal, Pierre kept brewing and never looked back.

Over the years, the beer grew in popularity, until Pierre's homebrewery was simply not large enough to accommodate. So he bought an old lemonade factory and converted it into his first full-scale brewery. Soon, Pierre's beers were not just a hit among fellow Belgians but also were beginning to become world renowned. During this time, Christine worked at the brewery sorting and washing beer bottles before she gradually stepped up to take on more administrative and exporting responsibilities. But things took a devastating turn for the Celis family in 1985, when the brewery suffered a damaging fire. When they did not have the funds to rebuild on their own, Belgian-based brewing conglomerate Interbrew (now part of the Anheuser-Busch InBev [AB InBev] beer autocracy) swooped in to help the Hoegaarden brewery rise from the ashes. The brewery experienced explosive growth; new, state-of-the-art equipment was installed, and renovations upped capacity exponentially. Hoegaarden was becoming a household name. In 1989, Pierre, then sixty-five, decided to retire from Hoegaarden. But that didn't mean he was ready to get out of the brewing game for good—not even close. It was then that Pierre asked Christine if she wanted to take a leap of faith and move to Texas. Ready to expand her horizons beyond the small Belgian village, Christine's answer was an emphatic yes.

The Celises were drawn to Austin for a bevy of reasons. For one, they heard the water was similar to the water in Hoegaarden because it was filtered through limestone. They also knew that there was not a single other brewery in Austin at the time, and with a large student population, people in the town definitely liked to go out, have a good time and drink some beer. From a strategic standpoint, Austin is smack-dab in the middle of the country, making both East and West Coast distribution easier than if it were marooned on one seaboard. Because Austin is only a few hours from the Gulf of Mexico, Pierre also dreamed about being able to export beer by ship back to Belgium one day. While all these reasons made sense from a tactical sales standpoint, Pierre was also drawn to Texans because they tend to talk slower than average Americans, a real necessity when English is your second language.

In 1990, Pierre bought a plot of land off Highway 290, a bit outside the hustle and bustle of the city back then. That next year, they started construction on what would become Austin's first brewery in nearly a century. Because Pierre never got a green card and his wife remained in Belgium, he would travel back and forth between the two countries frequently. Christine, on the other hand, filed for a green card and permanently moved to Austin to manage the upcoming Celis Brewery. On March 19, 1992, they brewed their first batch of beer; the endeavor took a full twenty-four hours. On May 1 of that year, they sold their very first case of the new flagship witbier, Celis White.

Getting Austinites to take a chance on Celis White was a bit of an uphill battle at first. Besides a few beer geeks who were drinking Chimay, Duvel and Hoegaarden, most Texans had never tasted a Belgian beer before.

"We had to educate people," Christine said. "People were very unfamiliar with a cloudy wheat beer; they had no idea."

The Celis approach was to win customers over one by one by getting them to appreciate the history and craftsmanship behind each beer. They did this by throwing events and tastings all over the city and inviting Austinites out to the brewery for tours and concerts. Their approach worked so well that, just like those early years in Hoegaarden, the brewery experienced rapid growth. The brewery's beer also garnered its fair share of critical praise, with Celis White taking home a host of Great American Beer Festival (GABF) and World Beer Cup medals over the years. Celis's other beers, including their Dubbel, Pale Rider, Grand Cru, Raspberry and Pale Bock, became very popular too, although none ever topped the success of Celis White.

By 1995, Celis was putting out twenty-three thousand barrels of beer per year and distributing to thirty states, making it the fastest-growing microbrewery in the United States at the time. But any meteoric rise comes with its fair share of growing pains, and Celis was certainly not immune to this truism.

As if beer weren't enough of a draw, Celis Brewery brought Austinites out with the lure of live music. *Ted Davis.*

"We couldn't follow our demand any more," Christine said. "We were like three months behind in production and people were getting upset. Distributors had to wait, and retailers would have an empty space for months...of course they were getting upset about it."

Considering the brewery had only been around for a few years at this point, the finances were certainly not there to pay for a full-scale brewhouse expansion so soon. So there, waiting in the wings like Marlon Brando, with an offer Celis couldn't refuse, was Miller Brewing Company. They offered to form a partnership with Celis to help it meet its production demands in exchange for an ownership stake in the company. It was a difficult decision for Pierre and Christine to make, but ultimately they decided that it seemed like the best path.

"We thought, well, maybe this will work out great," Christine said.

That optimism soon led Celis Brewery to win the leading role in a classic cautionary tale. After the first year, Miller pulled Celis out of twenty-five states in their thirty state distribution zone and pressured them to tweak their recipes to become more commercially viable.

"We were like, wait a minute, this is not what we signed up for," Christine said.

They also had to use only Miller distributors.

"A lot of the Miller distributors didn't even want it [Celis beer] because they weren't familiar with it," Christine said. "The bread and butter was the Miller beers, Celis was still that weird animal out there that they didn't know what to do with. They didn't know how to sell it."

The cubicle dwellers over at Miller headquarters were not any better.

"Big breweries are bankers," Christine said. "It's not about the passion [for] brewing, it's about 'How much money can we make with this?' It just didn't work out. It just wasn't a good deal for us at all."

The Celis team was so beat down by all the compromises it had to make that when Miller offered to buy the brewery outright in 2000, they didn't know what else to do but cut their loses and surrender. After all, it had become something very different from Pierre's original American dream.

"We were so sick and tired of dealing with a big corporation," Christine said. "It was sad. Why fix something that isn't broken. They messed with the whole thing. It wasn't Celis Brewery any more. So we sold it, and a year later, they closed down the brewery and said they had to focus on their Miller products."

In 2002, Miller sold the Celis name and brewing equipment to Michigan Brewing Company, which began brewing what many people argued were lower quality clones of the original Celis beers. Let's not forget, this was the same brewery that would later be responsible for brewing Kid Rock's American Badass Beer. The whole experience made Christine so mad that she decided to leave the brewing industry all together. She spent a few years staying at home with her kids, and she bought a Harley-Davidson to tool around the Texas Hill Country. It would be a few years before she even thought about setting foot in a brewery again, but eventually, she found her way back. Christine worked for a brewing equipment manufacturer before starting an importing company to bring beer from small, artisanal Belgian breweries to the United States.

Pierre Celis passed away in 2011 at the age of eighty-six. Before he died, Christine promised him that she would not give up until she had taken back the rights to their family name. Pierre's passing came just one year before Christine actually succeeded in this quest. Now, Christine plans to honor her father's memory by brewing his recipes again right here in Austin.

"We're not giving up," Christine said. "I think brewing was our destiny, and we're going to brew no matter what the odds are. We've always had a lot of obstacles, but it makes you stronger, it makes you better and it makes you much more careful too."

More information about the upcoming Pierre Celis Brewery can be found in chapter eight.

HILL COUNTRY BREWING CO.

From 1993 to 1999, Hill Country Brewing and Bottling Co., started by brothers Mike and Marshall McHone, produced a number of beers that were deemed by renowned beer critic Michael Jackson (no, not that Michael Jackson) to be faultless. That's quite a compliment for a brewery that began when Marshall, once a distributor for Shiner, approached his brother and said, "If you can make beer, I can sell it." Mike agreed to his brother's request and started looking into the process of brewing beer.

They bought a facility at 730 Shady Lane, only a few blocks from Live Oak Brewing's building. In their first year of brewing, they crafted the Balcones Fault Red Granite, brewed with British malts and English yeast that had a slight hop bitterness, and sold around 500 barrels. The other beer they brewed was Balcones Fault Pale Malt, a British-style pale ale. They depended on volunteers, a group of mainly homebrewers, friends and family. In the last couple years of Hill Country Brewing Co.'s life, the brewery usually made around 7,500 barrels annually. Most of its equipment came from various national, regional and microbreweries across the country, and its brewhouse utilized old dairy equipment along with a 1940s bottling line.

While the brewery was in operation, a percentage of sales for Balcones Fault Beers was donated to the Hill Country Foundation, a group that is dedicated to preserving Texas's beautiful Hill Country and the species of plants and animals indigenous to the region. Once Hill Country Brewing shut down, mainly due to the McHones' inability to keep up financially with an increasingly competitive market, Mike went into real estate, and Marshall now owns the White Horse, a honky-tonk in the thick of hipster bars, on Fifth and Comal Streets.

THE RISE OF BREWPUBS

Texas was incredibly late to the game when it came to brewpub licenses. A good forty-one states had already legalized them before Texas got the ball rolling. These licenses allow bars and restaurants to brew and sell their beer on site. A brewpub differs from production breweries because production breweries sell the majority of their beer in stores or bars off-site. A critical moment for the Austin craft beer scene came when

HB 1425 passed on September 1, 1993, during Texas's seventy-third legislative session. Introduced by Billy Forrester, who owned Dog & Duck Pub at the time and would go on to own Waterloo Brewing and Billy's on Burnet, the bill permitted brewpub licenses, and it passed without any naysayers.

"It's amazing to me that Texas took so long to [legalize brewpubs]," Draught House Pub & Brewery brewer and manager Josh Wilson said. "Because Texans love anything Texas."

"Distributors didn't care," North By Northwest owner Davis Tucker said. "As recently as two years ago, I heard a distributor say, 'Oh, craft beer's a fad.'"

Before brewpub licenses were legalized, there were not many active breweries in Texas. Spoetzl Brewery in Shiner was one of only a few breweries to make it past Prohibition and extend into the '90s and beyond. Efforts to expand the number of Texas breweries included some attempts to convince the Texas legislature to legalize brewpub licenses. Tucker helped to spearhead such an effort, which brought a bill before the legislature in 1987 that would legalize brewpub licenses. Unfortunately, the bill was tabled, and Tucker was told it was dropped completely.

"There had been...many attempts...to legalize brewpubs, and Billy decided that he wanted to do it," Steve Anderson, former head brewer for Waterloo Brewing Co., said.

With the passage of HB 1425, the brewpub scene exploded in Austin. Brian "Swifty" Peters remembers trying to start a brewpub in 1993 with Chip McElroy, now of Live Oak. By the time he and McElroy had finished their business plan, three or four brewpubs were already opening.

"It was hard to find the brewer/owner in the first wave," Peters said. "It was people who were thinking that brewpubs were a good business idea, and they brought in brewers."

Around eighteen brewpubs opened in Texas in the wake of HB 1425's passing. Within the next couple years, however, some of the original brewpubs closed due to inconsistent beer, beginner's mistakes and competition from big-name breweries such as Spoetzl and Anheuser-Busch.

"The margins early on are slim," Wilson said. "It takes a lot of work. You really have to be dedicated. Some people didn't realize that then, so they weren't willing to do what it takes to make it work. Also, a lot of people were just making really bad beer."

Brewpubs like Armadillo Brewing and Stone House Brewing slowly died out. Armadillo became the bar Katie Bloom's for a brief period before closing entirely, while Stone House became Boar's Head Pub, and the building they were in is now an Opal Divine's.

"A lot of people bit off more than they could chew," Anderson said. "There were a lot more [brewpubs] than people were willing to support, and a lot of them went under. It was pretty dry in Austin for a while before we started seeing breweries build in popularity."

By 1994, the Statistical and Information Services at the Beer Institute found that Texas was the top beer-producing state; by 1995, Texas had thirty-one brewpubs. Unlike their underprepared counterparts, certain Austin brewpubs—Waterloo, Bitter End Brewpub and Copper Tank Brewing Co.—flourished throughout the '90s and became craft beer meccas in Austin. However, despite pouring sweet, sweet beer, these brewpubs would not be around forever.

WATERLOO BREWING

Waterloo Brewing Co., a nod to Austin's original name, was the first brewpub to open in the city. Billy Forrester opened Waterloo in December 1993 (just three months after HB 1425 passed). Originally located at 401 Guadalupe, the brewpub quickly made a name for itself in Austin's beer scene.

"Billy was responsible for helping to legalize [brewpubs], so it was only appropriate that he opened the first brewpub in the state," Steve Anderson, Waterloo's head brewer, said.

The brewpub had three floors. The first floor contained the brewery and the restaurant, which sold mostly pub food—nachos, sandwiches and burgers—at very reasonable prices. The second floor housed a game room, and the third was a rooftop deck with a view of the West End entertainment district. The food and the prospect of lunch beers made Waterloo a desirable spot.

"Everyone went to Waterloo," Brian Peters said.

The beers that Waterloo brewmaster Anderson produced were all named after people and places from Austin's history, tying into the theme of the Waterloo name. Ed's Best Bitter, named after former Austin mayor Edwin Waller, was an English bitter that was low in carbonation and low in alcohol. Waterloo was one of the few breweries in Texas brewing an English bitter. O. Henry's Porter, which was named for short-story author William Sydney Porter, was an American-style porter that had more chocolate flavor than coffee. The decision to add a porter to the bar's beer lineup came from a personal request from Forrester's wife. Clara's Clara was a golden ale that was light and dry and paid homage to Clara Driscoll, an Austin resident who helped to preserve the Alamo Mission. Finally, Guytown IPA, named after Austin's red-light district that Waterloo Brewing once occupied, was a super-hoppy American-style IPA.

"We didn't have much competition really, so everyone was allowed to do more creative things," Anderson said. "In the end we had brewed about fifty different beers."

Waterloo Brewing Co. won multiple medals at Great American Beer Festivals during the years it was in operation. Samuel Houston's Austin Lager won silver in the Vienna Lager category in 1995. The next year, O. Henry's Porter won silver in the Robust Porter category. Waterloo's Prairie Dog Pils won bronze in the Bohemian-style Pilsner category in 1998. The last medal the brewery won was a gold in 1999 with their Waterloo Grand Cru.

The company closed in August 2001 due to rising property values and a lack of revenue. In tune with a current Austin trend, the building was converted into lofts and retail stores.

"Waterloo closing was a huge loss," Brian "Swifty" Peters said.

Many brewpubs would follow in Waterloo's footsteps.

Forrester would go on to open the craft beer–focused dive Billy's on Burnet, while Anderson would become a head brewer at Live Oak Brewing Co., before moving to Alpine, Texas, in 2012 to open Big Bend Brewing Co.

Bitter End Bistro and Brewery

Opened in 1994 by Reed and Betty Clemens at 311 Colorado Street, Bitter End Bistro and Brewery was widely regarded as a fantastic, upscale gastropub with highly lauded food and beer, and it even had a waiting list when it first opened. With a classier atmosphere than some of the other brewpubs, the Bitter End made a name for itself.

In addition to the main bar and restaurant, the Bitter End had a lounge in the basement of the Spaghetti Warehouse next-door to the brewpub called the B-Side. It was a bar that served Bitter End's beers along with a more laid-back atmosphere than the Bitter End.

"It was a great place to hide and hang out with your friends," Peters said.

Bitter End's then-brewmaster Tim Schwartz (right) raises a glass with legendary beer writer Michael Jackson (left) at the brewpub's second annual Dinner & Brew event in 2000. *Kathy Towns.*

The top floor of the B-Side became unofficially known by some as Little Amsterdam, and that's where people would go to do, well, things you would do in Amsterdam.

The Bitter End generally had five regular beers on tap, along with a couple of rotating taps. The beers you could expect to see included EZ Wheat, a light wheat beer that was its best seller; Aberdeen Amber, a Scottish-style ale with peat-smoked malt; Bitter End Bitter, an English-style extra special bitter that used English hops and malt with an American base; Fog City Lager, a San Francisco-style steam beer that was hoppier and fruitier than a regular lager; and Austin Pale Ale, its hoppiest brew and similar in taste to an India pale ale.

Many agree that one of the Bitter End's best decisions was hiring Tim Schwartz, who started off homebrewing and then began to win competitions around Austin. He also brewed a beer at Waterloo Brewing Co. in 1994. Schwartz started as a brewing assistant when the Bitter End first hired him; after only three months of working there, Schwartz was promoted to head brewer.

Once Schwartz took over brewing, the Bitter End won a variety of medals at the Great American Beer Festival. Bitter End's Prescott's Wee Heavy won medals in the Strong Scotch Ale category three years in a row from 1998 to 2000. It won again in 2002, and Lip Burner Lamb-Beak won silver in the Belgian-style Sour Ale category that same year. Sour Prick won bronze in that same category in 2004.

Schwartz was, and still is, known for embracing unconventional brewing techniques. In 2004, when he decided to experiment with brewing beers with soft water, he landed on the idea of using rainwater collected in Dripping Springs. Together with Richard Heinichen, owner of Richard's Rainwater, he crafted storm-fueled suds such as the Environmental Pale Ale and the Poindexter Pils.

After a promising career at the Bitter End, Schwartz left to pursue work at Real Ale Brewing. Peters, who left Live Oak Brewing in the early 2000s and began brewing under Schwartz at Bitter End, was promoted to head brewer once Schwartz left.

The Bitter End's closing was incredibly tragic. On August 21, 2005, a three-alarm fire devastated the building. No patrons were in the building at the time, and none of the staff was harmed. It started in the kitchen and eventually made its way to the roof of the building. Part of the roof ended up collapsing onto the kitchen and brewery. Bitter End's B-Side was unharmed and stayed open.

Peters had to go into the cold room to keg up the beer that survived the fire. To do so, he had to wade through all the water left behind by the fire hoses.

"We kegged up as much beer as we could and ran the beer to the B-Side," Peters said.

In the few months after the fire, Clemens tried to keep Bitter End afloat, and many believed that the brewpub would reopen.

"I did," Peters said. "But I'm an optimist."

Clemens told Peters to look into getting newer equipment along with better fermenters for the brewery. Bitter End was not only going to return but also do so with new, upgraded equipment. Hopes for a comeback were so high that the Bitter End even took its beer to the Great American Beer Festival that year.

Unfortunately, Clemens decided it wasn't cost effective to rebuild Bitter End, so the brewpub and the B-Side closed for good. Peters worked odd jobs after the Bitter End closed. He worked for Maine Root, making draft root

In a cosmic act of irony, a calamitous three-alarm fire broke out at the Bitter End Bistro and Brewery in 2005, and the venue never reopened. *Kathy Towns.*

beer, and did electrical work for Real Ale. Peters felt that this was a really low point in his life, going from brewing beer at Bitter End to brewing root beer. But he ended up getting offered a job at Uncle Billy's Brew and Que and worked there for several years before starting Austin Beer Garden Brewing Co. (see chapter eight for more on ABGB).

COPPER TANK BREWING CO.

Opened in June 1994 at 504 Trinity, Copper Tank Brewing Co. was named for the brilliant, beautiful copper tanks that its beer was brewed in. From the bar, patrons could gaze at the tanks and were given an inside look into what made Copper Tank tick.

Davis Tucker's, one of Copper Tank's coowners, path to beer happened in a very roundabout way. He studied government and international affairs and wanted to work at the Capitol—not the Texas Capitol, the nation's.

Before going to Washington, Tucker took a trip to Germany, where he fell in love with German beer. Tucker turned in his suit and tie and told his boss in Washington that he was going to open a beer company. When Tucker moved back to Austin, he immediately started his beer plans.

Copper Tank was called "stylish" and quickly became a favorite in Austin. It made around 124,000 gallons of beer (more than any other brewpub in Texas) while in production and had around four mainstay beers. Tucker, who ended up leaving Copper Tank in 1996, mostly worked with head brewer Rob Cartwright in the brewery to craft a variety of styles for Austinites. After the first year, Copper Tank opened a kitchen in which the chefs utilized the brewpub's beer in a lot of the food they offered, including menu staples like queso con cerveza (queso made with chilies and White Tail ale), French onion beer soup (French onion soup that added Big Dog brown ale to the mix) and beer batter onion rings.

Copper Tank was known for a variety of beers: Copper Light, an American-style ale that was the brewpub's bestselling beer, which sold around five hundred gallons a week; River City raspberry ale, an alteration to the Copper Light recipe with the addition of fresh raspberries; Big Dog brown ale, an English-style ale that had a lower ABV and slightly sweet, chocolate flavor; and finally, the Cliffhanger Alt, a German-style brown ale that was more bitter and hoppy than the Big Dog. Copper Tank won multiple awards at GABF during its lifetime, including silver in 1996 for its Cliffhanger Alt.

The Copper tank was a popular brewpub until it closed its doors in 2005. *Dan Dewberry.*

In 1997, it won silver for its Fall Fest Honey rye ale (which won silver again in 1998) and Copper Tank Vienna lager. The next year, it won gold for Mocha Madness. Then, in 2000, it won gold for Fuzzy Buzz peach ale.

Unfortunately, things started taking a turn for the worse for Copper Tank. Tucker felt that by selling the beers at a ridiculously low price, Copper Tank invited in rowdy bunches of college kids, who were not the type of people Copper Tank brewed for. They weren't there to enjoy the beer. They just liked the fact that it was cheap alcohol. He believed that these unsavory people drove away some of the true Copper Tank fans.

"In my mind, it was the death of Copper Tank that on Wednesday night was dollar pint night," Tucker said.

In 2005, the brewery closed due to bankruptcy. Many, including Tucker, felt that the closing also came about due to a poor location. Copper Tank was in an area where new, fad bars popped up every three months only to be shut down and remodeled into a newer fad bar. It was not the sort of area people went to sit down for some delicious craft beer. Others speculate that it closed because of mismanagement—a combination of focusing exclusively on the beer and not harmonizing the kitchen with the brewery—that killed Copper Tank. Copper Tank's beautiful tanks were taken by the bankruptcy liquidation process and were auctioned off. Now, the Copper Tank space is sometimes used for events, and its biggest claim to fame is that Justin Timberlake brought sexy back in a "Suit and Tie" for a 2013 South by Southwest appearance.

Lovejoys Tap Room and Brewery

Lovejoys opened its taps on 604 Neches Street in 1994. It was one of a handful of brewpubs to survive through the 1990s and into the late 2000s. Founded by Chip Tait, Lovejoys was initially a combination of a beer bar and coffee shop.

"We didn't really intend on brewing beer," Tait said.

Eric Roach and Darren White (owners of Austin Homebrew Supply at the time) wanted to convince Tait to start brewing at Lovejoys. So Roach and White created a plan on how they were going to set up a brewery in the bar and presented it to Tait. Tait said, "What the hell!" and flipped what was once a kitchen in the back of Lovejoys into a brewery. Roach and White did much of the brewing initially.

Eventually, however, the three realized that with Tait managing the bar and Roach and White owning Austin Homebrew Supply, it was becoming increasingly difficult to brew. So as Tait recalls, they stole an Austin Homebrew Supply employee named Paul Koonz and made him head brewer for Lovejoys. Koonz made some of Lovejoys first specialty beers, including Ol' Vixen, a barley wine brewed during the summer and aged in whiskey barrels. In conjunction with Ol' Vixen's tapping during the holiday season, Lovejoys would also run an Operation Blue Santa toy drive and would give a glass of Ol' Vixen to any patron who brought in a toy for the drive. Tait sometimes had to fill up his truck twice just to deliver all the toys.

"I was always amazed because our crowd at Lovejoys, it ran the gamut," Tait said. "There was a whole lot of people who came through there but generally a lot of them were broke-ass punks who liked good beer."

The brewpub quickly made a name for itself and became a local favorite—an oasis from the puke, frat boys and tequila shots that generally grace Sixth Street. There were usually around thirty taps, which included four rotating taps of the brewery's own beers. Some common terms that were used to describe Lovejoys included "grungy," "homey," "metal" and "punk rock."

Lovejoys brewed a hefty amount of beers during its eighteen years of business. Such beers included the AJ porter, an American-style porter; Samson's Best pale ale, named for owner Chip Tait's dog, an American pale ale that was dry and hoppy; Sparky's Special ale, an amber that was mildly sweet with a bitter finish; and Franciscan, one of Lovejoys's most popular beers (one time, even special ordered for a wedding ceremony), a Belgian-style brown ale that was brewed with Belgian-style yeast that gave it a rich, not-too-sweet flavor.

In 2006, Chip Tait sold Lovejoys to Eric Wolf. Tait decided he was done with the brewpub business and wanted to move on. He had two offers on Lovejoys. The first one came from someone who Tait believed to be a businessman who would just rip down the building and put something else in its place. The other was from Wolf. Despite not being a regular, Wolf was more interested in retaining Lovejoys's character and continuing what Tait built.

Despite Wolf's good intentions and hard work, Lovejoys had to close shop in August 2012. It was unable to keep up with the rising rent at its Sixth Street location and was experiencing a decrease in revenue. Wolf said that, at some point, Lovejoys might resurface and hinted that he could possibly relocate the restaurant to a more affordable location. Only time will tell if Lovejoys will return.

Draught House Pub and Brewery

Draught House, which was opened in 1968 by Wayne Overton and his wife, Gay, started off as a single-family home that Overton bought, ripped down and rebuilt as a tavern. He wanted to run a multitap tavern, a practically unheard of concept during the '60s. Done in a similar style to the Tavern (that place on Twelfth and Lamar with the air conditioning), Draught House has an old-school tavern or beer garden feel. The inside is a little dim and features a lot of dark woodwork, but it feels cozy and is the sort of place you'd meet your friends for a pint. A side patio with tons of seating, along with the occasional food truck, completes the beer garden image.

In the 1990s, after Wayne had died, Gay was running the place. Her health deteriorated, and eventually, Josh Wilson and Dan Moran bought the tavern from her and reopened the Draught House, renaming it Draught Horse due to Gay's desire that they not use the original name. Then, in

Although the Draught House opened in 1968, it didn't begin brewing beer until the mid-1990s. *Kat McCullough.*

1994, they installed the brewing equipment that set Draught Horse on the brewing path and started brewing in 1995.

"We made money the first day we opened our doors," Wilson said. "We've always had a problem with keeping up with demand because we're so restricted by our system size and our building size. So we're always running out of beer—since day one."

Located at 4112 Medical Parkway in Austin's Rosedale neighborhood, Draught Horse became a favorite local spot and is well respected for the seventy beers it has on tap. At the bar, you can expect to see a range of patrons, from people who have been fans for twenty years to first-time customer. One story tells of a father coming to Draught Horse to show his son where he'd scratched his name on a table in the '70s.

Eventually, Wilson and Moran's partnership dissolved. They sold Draught Horse to Glenda Smith, who runs a dentistry business next door, and Wilson stayed on as head brewer. By this point, Gay Overton had passed, and Smith changed the name back to Draught House.

Since Draught House has seventy taps, Wilson is able to focus on experimenting in seven-barrel batches and doesn't have to worry about producing a beer for the masses.

"I don't have to brew beers that I know are going to sell fast," Wilson said. "So I can be experimental."

Beers that are included in the bar's repertoire include its vanilla porter, an American porter with notes of chocolate and vanilla; Golden Hour, a hefeweizen that is citrusy and wheaty; and Red Planet, an American amber that is hoppy and malty.

REAL ALE BREWING

Real Ale Brewing Co. opened in July 1996 on the Austin outskirts in a little town called Blanco. Philip, Diane and Charles Conner were the initial owners of the brewery, which was set up in an antique store's basement.

"[It was] quaint but really tough to brew in," current director of brewing operations Tim Schwartz said.

Around 1998, Philip Conner decided he wanted to get out of the brewing business. He asked Brad Farbstein, a homebrewer and Real Ale volunteer, if he knew anyone willing to take over Real Ale. Farbstein knew just the guy—himself. Although Farbstein was young and not exactly a wealthy venture capitalist, he worked out a deal with the Conners, and that summer, he took over Real Ale. With the help of two employees, Farbstein pumped out 500 barrels of beer that year (now they sell around that much in a day). Eventually, the brewery outgrew its original location, brewing nearly 5,500 barrels a year, which, let's be real, is extremely impressive considering these guys were brewing in a basement. Around 2000, Erik Ogershok started work for Real Ale and became the brewery's brewmaster. In 2006, Farbstein purchased several acres of land and transplanted Real Ale from its original location to a new facility that is able to keep up with its popularity. Even with a 60-barrel system, along with a newer and bigger facility, Real Ale took a while to catch up to the demand it had for its beer.

"We caught up with demand last summer," Schwartz said. "[The new facility] allowed us to catch up [which we wanted] because we were running very low across the state."

The first three beers that Real Ale brewed during those first few years included the Brewhouse Brown, a rich, roasty brown ale that has slight hints

(From left to right) Real Ale's Brent "Schmitty" Sapstead, Erik Ogershok and Tim Schwartz celebrate the brewery's seventeenth anniversary in May 2013. *Holly Aker.*

Brad Farbstein (left) poses with his father, Jack Farbstein (right), at the original Real Ale brewhouse. *Brad Farbstein.*

Real Ale owner Brad Farbstein brewed in his brewhouse during his first year as owner. *Brad Farbstein.*

Real Ale Brewing Company has come a long way since it started in the basement of an antique shop in Blanco's town square. *Holly Aker.*

of chocolate and a dry finish; Rio Blanco pale ale, an English-style pale ale that has a spicy hop flavor that won gold at the Great American Beer Festival in 2010; and Full Moon Pale Rye Ale, which balances the sweetness of the malted rye and barley with a generous amount of hops.

In addition to the beers listed above, Real Ale has recently started bottling and canning its Hans Pilz, a beer you may recognize as the pairing for this chapter. Real Ale has been brewing Hans Pilz for around three years and, in 2012, started bottling it.

"When we put it out draft only, it was one of the fastest-selling beers we had," Ogershok said.

Hans Pilz went on to win the silver medal at GABF in 2012.

The beer that Real Ale is best known for is Firemans #4, a blonde ale that is citrusy, thirst quenching and not overbearing like that blanket of Austin humidity you'll most likely be wrapped in while drinking it. It won silver at the Great American Beer Festival in 2012. The beer became very popular and has been a gateway beer for many a nonbeer drinker.

"Even before we put it in the bottle, it was our main seller," Schwartz said.

Thanks to the growth Real Ale has experienced, it has been able to begin a number of projects. It has gone from about five hundred barrels a year to five hundred barrels a day. Real Ale has started bottling a lot of its seasonals, including Coffee Porter and Devil's Backbone, a Belgian-style tripel. Devil's Backbone quickly became popular enough to be made all year long.

In the past few years, Real Ale has been able to start a barrel program and has begun barrel aging beer. The program, named Mysterium Verum (translated to "real mystery"), is something that Ogershok and Schwartz had been wanting to start for some time.

"There's probably been six months in the history of this brewery since I've been working here that we haven't been under construction," Ogershok said. "During that period, we got our first four barrels and filled them. That was the beginning of Mysterium Verum."

These first four barrels included two barley wines and a Scotch ale. Since those first barrels, the beers in the Mysterium Verum program have grown and can range from just barrel aging a Real Ale seasonal to an entirely new creation that has been aged in either wood or stainless steel or a combo of both. Since each beer comes out of the barrels different from the last batch, Real Ale started renaming each batch.

"We don't want the beer to be judged by its former self," Ogershok said.

The names Real Ale picks for these beers are also seriously epic. Names include Highlander, which makes sense since there can be only one, Scots

Gone Wild, Shipwrecked and the Kraken, which was released (#GetIt?) in 2013.

Real Ale continues to grow and expand on the types of projects it can do. Since updating its system and facility, Real Ale can produce somewhere between 54,000 and 72,000 barrels a year. This is a massive step up from the 5,500 barrels it did during its first year in the business. With Mysterium Verum and the increasing demand for its beer, the Real Ale's future is looking pretty bright.

LIVE OAK BREWING COMPANY

Conceptualized in 1994, Live Oak Brewing Company was officially opened in 1997 by homebrewers Chip McElroy and Brian "Swifty" Peters and has become a staple in the Austin beer scene. McElroy first got the taste for beer when he was in graduate school in the '80s. Jokes aside about graduate students drinking a lot, McElroy and his peers would throw huge parties and fill a baby wading pool with beer.

In the 1980s, he developed a serious love for pilsners and lagers when he lived in Europe for ten months. But McElroy's path to becoming a brewer himself began when he attended a biochemistry conference in Colorado. While attending the conference, McElroy met a man who lived in San Diego and was really into homebrewing. McElroy, knowing he was planning on going to San Diego to do research in molecular biology, began chatting with this guy, and they got to the subject of brewing beer.

"I really learned how to brew with him," McElroy said.

Three years later, once McElroy had finished his research, he returned to Austin, joined the Austin Zealots and then met Peters, who shared McElroy's love for Czech-style pilsners. The two started brewing together. They would meet at Peters's house and brew to their heart's content. At the time, McElroy had a lousy stove in his place and great homebrewing equipment while Peters had an excellent stove and no homebrewing equipment. It was a match made in brewing heaven. Generally, the two would brew German styles of beer that other homebrewers and even small breweries weren't making.

"So we started making good beer and people started saying, 'You should start selling this,'" McElroy said.

Initially, McElroy and Peters considered starting a brewpub. They found that it was a lot more work than they'd thought. They both realized that they had no experience in the restaurant aspect of brewpubs, which is half the equation. Neither of them was a great cook (despite whipping up some tasty beers), and they both decided that this wasn't the path for them.

"We'd hired this guy to be our consultant, but it was just too much," McElroy said. "So we decided to just do a brewery, and then it all kind of fell into place. I can't cook, and I don't really care what sauce goes on the asparagus."

During the initial process of marketing their beer, McElroy and Peters would drive around Austin to different craft beer bars and try to get them to buy it. Initially, they were told there was no way in hell the bar would buy their beer. Eventually, though, they reached a point when their beers were selling, and they decided to take the next step. McElroy and Peters bought a small piece of a building on 3301 East Fifth Street.

"The place was pretty much a derelict building and [our] side was what [our neighbors] called 'the Dark Side.' It had been burned partially, and all the wiring and metal had been stripped out of it," McElroy said.

With the help of Dave Reggler, who is still good friends with McElroy and Peters to this day, they built their brewing facility from the ground up. They replumbed the building, fixed multiple electrical problems, poured cement and truly overhauled the space. Dave Reggler had a background in construction, and Peters and McElroy knew what they wanted for Live Oak's facility; the project was completed in a year.

Live Oak's beers have gone on to win numerous awards, including the silver medal in the 2012 World Beer cup for its Primus. The name hints at something epic, and Primus lives up to it. Primus is a weizenbock, which is a winter seasonal that is malty and spicy. Their HefeWeizen is extremely popular in Austin and is particularly coveted nationwide—it is light and refreshing during the hot Austin summers with a strong banana character.

"Back in '97, it was hard to give the [the HefeWeizen] away," McElroy said. "Nowadays, I believe it has officially taken over our top-selling spot."

Live Oak's arsenal of beers is great for any kind of situation you might find yourself in, such as catching a movie at the Alamo Drafthouse. One pitcher of Live Oak HefeWeizen, and you are golden. But the HefeWeizen isn't the brewery's only approachable, easy-drinking offering. Live Oak Pilz is a crisp pilsner that is both hoppy and smooth with a dry finish. Big Bark Amber Lager is a Vienna-style lager with little hop bitterness and a malty flavor. Live Oak describes it as "all bark, no bite." Liberation Ale has strong, hoppy notes with a sixty on the International Bittering Units (IBU) scale, and Live Oak says that it is one of the most well-balanced IPAs you will ever have.

Live Oak
HefeWeizen is
one of the most
ubiquitous beers in
Austin. *Shaun Martin.*

Live Oak Brewing Co. has maintained high sales despite the fact that its beer is only available on tap. Its beers are so popular in Austin that many (including most of the authors of this book) have lamented the fact that the company doesn't bottle yet. It has plans for expansion, which can be read about in chapter eight.

NORTH BY NORTHWEST RESTAURANT AND BREWERY

Started in 1999 by Davis Tucker, North by Northwest Restaurant and Brewery (NXNW) stands as one of the few surviving brewpubs to open during the

'90s beer movement. NXNW is the culmination of Davis Tucker's love for German beer that started way back in 1984, along with Tucker's desire to follow his own ideas. He knew immediately after opening Copper Tank that he was not interested in a partnership and wanted to do his own thing.

"So I left [Copper Tank]," Tucker said. "And in September '99, I opened up NXNW."

Tucker set out on the ultimate beer quest to start his brewpub brainchild.

"NXNW came into existence from an idea that I had many years ago—that great craft-brewed beer and fabulous food could come together in a fun and interesting atmosphere," Tucker said.

The name came from the fact that Tucker wanted to pay homage to the Northwest, where many brewpubs and microbreweries started. NXNW offers growler fills and an upscale atmosphere. Tucker puts a lot of pride into providing the best brewpub experience out there and is passionate about making NXNW a fantastic food and beer experience. He believes that brewpubs cannot succeed if they focus solely on beer.

"I always say that you better be a damn good restaurant and make damn good beer," Tucker said. "The people come to the restaurant, especially North By, for an experience."

The majority of the beers that brewmaster Don Thompson (who helped Tucker build Copper Tank) and head brewer Kevin Roark (who worked at Bitter End) brew are inspired by the beers being brewed in the Northwest and German-style beers. Both of the brewers at NXNW have years of brewing experience and, with their malty powers combined, brew up some tasty creations. Beers that you can enjoy there include Northern Light, a lager brewed with Horizon hops and pilsner malts that makes for easy drinking while soaking up some sun on NXNW's patio. Duckabush Amber is a Vienna lager that is smooth, creamy and not overpowering. Blackjack Ale is a black ale that has been aged in Jack Daniel's whiskey barrels to create woody, roasty deliciousness.

NXNW is located at 10010 North Capital off Texas Highway and offers brunch, lunch and dinner, along with an extensive beer, wine and specialty drinks menu. There are also cask nights held on the last Monday of each month, which usually showcase some one-of-a-kind creation from Roark. The brewpub hosts beer classes on specific beer-related topics, such as beer and cheese or chocolate pairings, how beer is made, beer history and many others.

The beer movement of the 1990s set the groundwork for what would soon become a burgeoning beer community in the capital city. It not only educated Austin palates, but also opened the door for brewers to experiment

NXNW head brewer Kevin Roark brews Kodiak in the brewery's lovely copper system. *Debbie Cerda.*

with different styles and provide Austinites with the kinds of beer they wanted. At the time, brewers would band together to borrow ingredients from each other. The brewers at Lovejoys were good friends with the guys at Bitter End and would store some of Lovejoys's grain at Bitter End. All the brewers realized early on that, in order to survive, they needed to make good beer so they would not develop a bad name for the collective. This served to create friendlier competition and an overall sense of community within Austin's beer scene that continues on to this day.

CHAPTER FOUR
BYOB (BREW YOUR OWN BEER)

PAIRS WITH AUSTIN BEERWORKS BLACK THUNDER

HOMEBREWING HAS HISTORY

Homebrewing started long before the craft beer craze, the DIY movement or the belt-tightening recession. It started before President Obama brewed his honey ale, before Austin Homebrew Supply opened its doors, before the name Papazian held any meaning beyond a misspelled dog breed or kind of chair and even before President Carter legalized the stuff in 1978. Yes, from Ancient Egypt to Mesopotamia, practically since the dawn of agriculture, man (or more commonly in those days, woman) has been brewing beer in small batches for household consumption. So revered was the production of this beer, in fact, that the ancient Sumerians even had a goddess of brewing, Ninkasi.

Some of America's earliest settlers were homebrewers. They say the first beer to be brewed in the New World was in 1587 at Sir Walter Raleigh's colony in Roanoke, Virginia. However, a wealth of evidence suggests that Native Americans were brewing beer using maize far earlier. As with many of the earlier ancient cultures, brewing was an important household chore in colonial America and was largely performed by women. An 1850 census of Texas reveals that nineteen people in the state listed themselves as brewers or distillers, yet the same year's state manufacturing schedule listed zero breweries. This suggests that even though those individuals

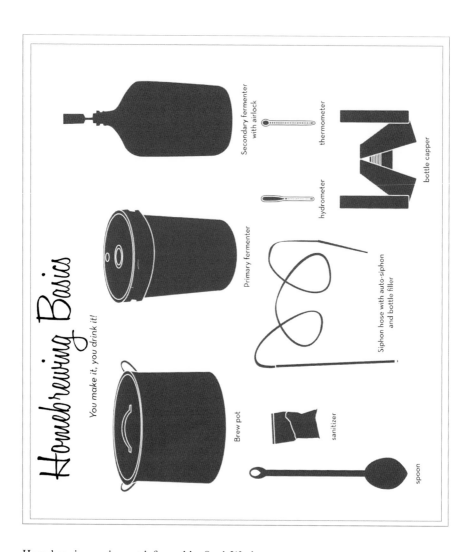

Homebrewing equipment infographic. *Sarah Wood.*

considered themselves brewers by trade, they were probably small home-based operations. When ratification of the Eighteenth Amendment was certified on January 16, 1919, homebrewing became illegal right along with for-profit alcohol production. Though the Twenty-first Amendment was passed in 1933, it did not repeal the ban on the homebrewing of beer. So homebrewing beer without taxation remained technically illegal in the United States for sixty stodgy years. Finally, in 1979, the Carter administration had the good sense to pass HR 1337, making brewing in small amounts for home consumption legal once again. Still, individual states had the power to override it, and it took until 2013, when Mississippi and Alabama finally went the way of the nation, to make homebrewing permissible in all fifty states. According to Texas law, an individual can now produce up to two hundred gallons of homebrew per year. That beer can be enjoyed for personal use and at organized tastings and gatherings as long as no fee is charged.

HOMEBREWING 101

Beer is of course composed of four basic ingredients—malt, hops, yeast and water. Add a bucket, a thermometer, some tubes and a few other odds and ends, and you can make it for yourself. A basic five-gallon, introductory homebrewing kit typically contains a plastic bucket to be used as a primary fermenter, a carboy for secondary fermentation, a stopper, airlocks, siphon hose, auto-siphon, clamp and bottle filler, bottle capper and caps, grain bag, hydrometer, thermometer, large spoon and some sanitizer. A stainless-steel brew pot is also essential. From there, experienced homebrewers can advance to brewing on propane-powered Cajun cookers and, eventually, larger pilot systems. Most avid homebrewers also move from bottling to kegging their beer, and from extract brewing to all grain brewing. If it sounds a little complicated, just remember, your reward will be some cold beer.

AUSTIN HOMEBREW SUPPLY

The year was 1990, and recent University of Iowa graduate Forrest Rogness was browsing the shelves of John's Grocery, a mom-and-pop grocery store turned Iowa City institution boasting one of the most toast-worthy beer selections in the Midwest. While deciding between the shop's wide array of Belgian, German, English and American brews, he spotted a beginner's homebrewing kit. In need of a new hobby, Forrest took the kit home with him, a decision that turned out to be life altering. It was kind of a banner year for him, because just months later, Forrest met his future wife, Diane, when they began working at a camera shop together. It was a true craft beer love story. She told him she was not a fan of beer. He responded, "You just haven't had the right one yet." Of course, Forrest soon won Diane over with some quality suds, and they became partners not only in life but also in brewing.

A year later, back here in Austin, a gentleman named Dave Bone founded Austin Homebrew Supply in a small converted house on East 53 ½ Street. After a few years, the shop changed hands. A few years after that, the later, originally enthusiastic, owners soon found themselves ready to move on.

Armed with a crude website and little storage space, Forrest, now living in Austin, was running an online mail-order homebrew supply business out of his garage called Rogness Homebrew Supply. He was also holding down a day job at Precision Camera. The online business ended up being a shocking success, bringing in approximately $30,000 in sales in the first year. As excited as Forrest was that his side project was making bank, he was, admittedly, exhausted. Having to fill the onslaught of orders during his off hours from Precision was getting less and less feasible, and it was becoming clear that he would have to choose between the two. Though Forrest got most of his inventory from a wholesaler, he was a frequent visitor of Austin Homebrew Supply. He got to know the owners, and he saw a serendipitous opportunity to take the shop off his friends' hands and combine his mail-order business with a storefront. We're guessing Diane was onboard with any plan that would get Forrest to clean out the garage.

"It was a risk, but it was a good move," Forrest said. "It turned out well."

Forrest followed his love of brewing, and he and Diane received the keys to AHS in 1999. They have been selling equipment for beer, wine and cheese making ever since, as well as offering a range of classes for beginner to expert level homebrewers. The shop has expanded and moved several times, and it currently occupies a warehouse space at 9129 Metric. One of the largest homebrew shops in the country, AHS sells more than 1,100 different recipe kits and thousands of ingredients for customers to customize their own recipes. Some of the equipment that AHS sells, like wort chillers, are actually manufactured in-house and sold through a major distributor to other homebrewing shops all over the country.

When Forrest took over at AHS, he was the sole employee. He ran the shop and the web business by himself until eventually hiring a second employee part time. Then, he added another and then another. Today, AHS employs around fifty people. Every employee ended up there in a different way.

Jon Airheart began working in the AHS shipping department in 2007 after deciding to leave his former shipping job at a large computer manufacturer.

"I had this epiphany when I was holding this box that was probably worth $100,000, and I was getting paid $10 an hour. And that wasn't cool to me," Airheart said. "And, a couple weeks later, I was getting paid the same thing pushing around a cart with $100 worth of stuff on it; I just felt better about myself."

Even though Airheart was working at AHS and was very involved in the founding of Black Star Co-op (a cooperatively owned brewpub that you can read all about in a later chapter), he had never tried his hand at homebrewing.

"I didn't want my hobby to also be homebrewing," he said. "But my employee discount was too good, and I had to eventually just get involved."

As Airheart's homebrewing knowledge began to grow and Forrest learned more about his employee's professional background, he saw potential in him and promoted him to store buyer. After two years, Airheart left AHS on a full-time basis. He still continues to work for Forrest at Rogness Brewing (which will also be covered in a later chapter) and helps manage social media for AHS.

Through his work at the shop, Airheart has had the opportunity to help out with some of the classes and provide guidance and support to new homebrewers.

"I tell people in class if your ambitions are to open a commercial brewery, we can help you along the way. But if you just want to bottle and do extract recipes your whole life, that's fine too. We're here for you," he said.

It's not just AHS customers who dream of starting breweries; many former employees have achieved that goal.

"Several local commercial brewers worked a stint at Austin Homebrew Supply while planning and financing their dream of opening a brewery," Airheart said.

Former employees have gone on to work at breweries such as Jester King, Bastrop Brewhouse and, of course, Rogness Brewing. As Forrest sees it, the homebrewing community and Austin's larger craft beer scene are intrinsically connected.

"The more craft beer [becomes] more prevalent, the more people want to homebrew, and then they want to become brewers," he said. "It keeps growing. It feeds on itself in a good way."

Whether homebrewers have aspirations of starting their own breweries or not, it doesn't come as much of a surprise that they end up being some of the biggest craft beer fans out there.

"Homebrewers are really on the front line of supporting craft beer and being craft beer advocates," homebrewer Dave Ebel said. "In a lot of ways, homebrewers are striving to aim for those goals. They want the ability to brew beers as good and as consistent as the commercial brewers, and the craft beer brewers are looking for the originality of what's coming out of the homebrew scene."

In fact, a number of local breweries are so interested in the beer being produced by homebrewers that they hold special pro-am competitions. In a typical pro-am competition, homebrewers (or amateur brewers) compete to have their beer brewed by a professional brewer, brewed on a professional system and/or distributed by a professional brewery. Flix Brewhouse has a rotating pro-am handle in which they feature recipes from local homebrewers brewed on the Flix system. Uncle Billy's Brew and Que holds a yearly pro-am competition. The winning beer is brewed commercially at Uncle Billy's and is entered in the Great American Beer Festival in Denver's pro-am competition.

ZEALOTS, MEDALS AND YELLOWISH HOPS

A zealot is typically defined as someone who is fanatical and uncompromising in his or her pursuits, but for the Austin "ZEALOTS," the city's largest homebrewing club, the moniker stands for "Zymurgic Enthusiasts of Austin Loosely Organized Through Suds." Well, maybe they are a little fanatical about that pursuit. The Zealots claim an official founding in 1994, though it's said that the group was actually even more loosely organized a few years earlier when a handful of homebrewing friends came together for occasional meetings at the Crown & Anchor and Dog & Duck pubs. In addition to some passionate homebrewers, the group of early founders also included the owners of Live Oak Brewing Co., the early owners of Austin Homebrew Supply and employees at Celis Brewery.

"The Zealots are a very loose group," Jon Airheart said. "So, if you've ever just homebrewed and been to a meeting, you're pretty much a Zealot."

Brian "Swifty" Peters became a Zealot that way in 1991, when he moved to Austin and started attending meetings at the Crown & Anchor Pub. He'd

The Zealots take a brewery tour while in San Diego for the 2011 National Homebrewers Conference. *Corey and Angela Martin.*

already been homebrewing for a couple years back in Indiana and quickly found camaraderie with the small group then led by AHS's Dave Bone. By the next year, Peters was president.

"Those were some of the best days, for me at least," Peters said. "I was able to meet a bunch of great brewers that way."

It was through the Zealots that Peters met homebrewers turned heavy hitter brewers Chip McElroy—with whom he would go on to start Live Oak Brewing Co.—and Tim Schwartz, who he would go on to brew with at the Bitter End. Peters and McElroy lived near each other in Travis Heights and soon became homebrewing partners. While at one fateful Oktoberfest homebrewing competition out in Walburg, Texas, Peters gained untold respect for Schwartz's brewing abilities.

"That's when I learned that Tim Schwartz brewed an Oktoberfest over an open fire," Peters said. "And he won; then, I realized he was the biggest badass brewer I've ever met—and still is."

Back when the Zealots' earliest members first started homebrewing in the late 1980s and first couple years of the '90s, there was no mecca for them like

Austin Homebrew Supply. They would buy their ingredients at grocery stores, such as Wheatsville Co-op. There, resourceful homebrewers could purchase dry yeast, individually canned Coopers extract, a few different grain options to make a mini mash and a handful of yellowish hop varieties sold in pellet or plug form. The ingredients were certainly nothing to write home about, a far cry from the vast array of ingredients and equipment available today at shops like AHS and the numerous well-stocked online retailers out there.

"It's easy to be a homebrewer now because the ingredients are great, the data is so good and the information is so good," Peters said. "We were pre-Internet. We were reading it out of books and not having good ingredients. So the homebrew shop brought in better and better ingredients to the point where anybody, as long as [he or she follows] the instructions really well, could make good beer."

By the mid-90s, Peters and McElroy were deep in the thralls of planning and building out Live Oak Brewing Co., so the Zealots soldiered loosely on under the new leadership of Steve Williams.

Being part of a homebrewing club, rather than going at it alone, holds many benefits for the Zealots. Zealots member Joe White (who is also president of another homebrewing club, the Texas Carboys) first joined because it was the only homebrewing club in town, and he wanted to meet some like-minded folks.

"Even after brewing for twenty years, I learn something new every time I see someone else brew," White said.

Airheart agrees.

"It's definitely about community and just learning—constantly learning," he said.

That learning benefits both individual homebrewers as well as the clubs they belong to. At a typical Zealots meeting, all the members bring a few bottles of homebrew for everyone to pass around and try. When Dave and Melissa Ebel attended their first Zealots meeting, they watched in dismay as another club member actually spit out their homebrew after the first sip. It wasn't exactly a rave review, but it did motivate them to work at becoming better brewers.

"Everybody likes to pat each other on the back, and everybody likes to give each other a good review; but it's the honest reviews that help you become a better brewer," Dave said. "Nobody starts off a phenomenal brewer. You've gotta learn, and you've gotta pay your dues."

The experience of seeing their beloved brew spit back up didn't traumatize the Ebels too much. In fact, when they attend Zealots meetings

The Zealots' cornhole set resides at the Rogness Brewing beer garden. *Holly Aker.*

these days, they often leave their homebrew unlabeled on a table and wait for people to pick it up. That way, they can watch others' honest reactions as they drink.

"You just stand by people and say, 'Oh, how is that one?' and they tell you the truth," Melissa said.

Today, these monthly meetings tend to draw between fifty and seventy attendees.

"We've really seen a huge growth in the number of people joining our e-mail list and coming to our meetings here in the last two years," Zealot Dan Dewberry said. "To the point that you used to be able to go to a meeting and know everyone's name no problem, and now, it's just impossible."

Dewberry credits the modern direction and consequent growth of the Zealots to former president Marc Martin, who moved to Austin in 1999:

In my opinion, the Zealots made a major turn when Marc Martin moved here [to Austin] from Portland, Oregon. He had been homebrewing for a real long time. And he saw how disorganized we were and still are. Within a few meetings, Steve Williams pretty much said, "You're totally into this; you need to be president of the Zealots." So he became president [or primary fermenter as they now call it] of the Zealots. He got us organized; he had us rating beers [and] scoring them. He really got us into entering contests and into going to the National Homebrewers Conference [NHC] *and into starting our own homebrewing contest, the Inquisition.*

The winners of the Inquisition are announced during the Zealots annual picnic, which is held every August at Emma Long Metropolitan Park in Northwest Austin. The event has grown so much that in recent years, it has boasted more than forty kegs of homebrew, brisket cook-offs and sometimes a full pig roast.

Corey Martin, who succeeded Marc Martin (no relation) as primary fermenter of the Zealots, got his first start at homebrewing when he was living in Whitney, Texas. At the time, homebrewing hadn't been legal for long, and Martin wasn't legal at all, considering he was not yet twenty-one. Since there's nothing shady about buying some hops, yeast and malt extract, Martin bought ingredients from a small grocery store and, together with a friend, set out to create his first beer. Since they were on the Brazos River, they dubbed their maiden voyage into the world of zymurgy "Brazos Brew." In what should have been a bit of a spoiler alert as to the outcome of Brazos Brew, the kit didn't even have a designated style.

"The ingredients were terrible," Martin said. "It just came out horrific."

Discouraged, Martin took a long break from homebrewing and didn't pick up the hobby again until years later, when he was serving in the air force and a friend brought in a homebrewing magazine (it could have been *Zymurgy* or *Brew Your Own* magazine—who can remember).

"I was entranced with that thing," Martin said. "It reignited my interest in it. I started up again then, and I haven't stopped. It's been twenty years."

After moving to Austin, Martin landed in with the Zealots pretty quickly. A friend found an advertisement in one of the local newspapers for the club's old monthly meetings at the Ginger Man pub and convinced him to go.

Martin said, "But, we don't know what we're doing," and his friend said, "Well, they don't either. Let's go."

This was in 1993 or 1994, though even back then, most of the early Zealots were pretty experienced homebrewers. But the meeting must have not been too intimidating because Martin and his wife, Angela, have been going ever since.

"We all have one thing in common, and that's homebrewing," he said. "We have people in our club who are doctors and lawyers, and we have blue-collar workers. It ranges. We're all equals because we're all homebrewers, and we love beer."

Today, Corey is known as much for his impressive homebrewing accolades as he is for his infectious laugh, which he developed trying to emulate the laugh track from *M*A*S*H* as a kid.

That signature giggle quickly turned into tears of joy one fateful morning in 2011, when Martin achieved something most homebrewers would only dream of: winning the Samuel Adams LongShot American Homebrew Contest. As a result, he got to see his winning recipe, a Munich-style dunkel, dubbed "A Dark Night in Munich," bottled commercially through Samuel Adams and available on shelves nationwide.

The announcement came at Samuel Adams's annual LongShot brunch on the Saturday morning of the Great American Beer Festival in Denver. After two days of sampling dozens and dozens of beers at the festival, Corey's stomach was in knots as he waited to find out his fate.

"I was suffering," he said. "[It was] half hangover, half nerves."

After the announcement (and the aforementioned tears of joy) came, Corey was in much higher spirits.

"It was a great honor," he said. "I mean, way cool."

For his first duty as a LongShot winner, Corey poured his beer to GABF attendees at both Saturday sessions. He did so in true Texan style.

"They said to dress business casual, and I thought, well, I don't have a lot of business casual shoes, so I'll wear my cowboy boots," Corey said. "Well, they're not very comfortable standing there for twelve hours straight. I was in so much pain by the end of that day."

A few months later, A Dark Night in Munich started popping up on shelves in the LongShot variety six-pack, complete with Corey's cartoon face on the label. Angela was so proud and excited that she started buying up cases and cases of the beer wherever she could find it.

"I finally had to tell her to stop buying it because I could make it cheaper," Corey said.

After the seasonal six-packs started to disappear from store shelves, Corey started to make a habit of rebrewing the beer, since friends and family who visit the Martins' house always clamored to try it. He tries to keep it on their eight-tap home kegerator at all times. Since his win, he has experimented with different yeast strains in the beer, but none of the deviations has ever beaten the taste of the original recipe.

"We've got ten refrigerators," Angela said, "and a very high electric bill."

"And I've got a very understanding wife," Corey said. "We've got them spread out on different circuit breakers."

The Martins are certainly not the only homebrewers with a rampant refrigerator habit. At Keith and Pam Bradley's Northwest Austin home, their two-car garage is adorned with full-size refrigerators, converted freezers, carboys and hoses. Name a piece of brewing equipment, and

Corey Martin pours his Samuel Adam's Longshot American Homebrew Contest beer, A Dark Night in Munich, at GABF in 2011. *Dan Dewberry.*

they will probably have plenty of it and the medals to go with—lots and lots of medals. In their twenty years of homebrewing, they've medaled at competitions all over the country, including right here in Texas.

Started in 2006, the Lonestar Circuit is the pinnacle of Texas homebrewing. The competition's three awards (Individual Winner, Team Winner, Club Winner) are given out based on a tallying of points from nine major homebrewing competitions around the state, beginning with the Bluebonnet Brew-Off in March and culminating with the Dixie Cup in October. The Bradleys are members of both the Austin Zealots and the Texas Carboys but tend to compete in the Lonestar Circuit as Zealots because they've been members of the club for thirteen years. The Zealots didn't make much of a splash in the first four years of the circuit, which was always won by either the Foam Rangers or the Bay Area Mashtronauts. All that changed in 2010.

"All of a sudden, a lot of us started garnering medals," Keith said. "When the Zealots won the Lonestar Circuit in 2010, it seemed like a lot of the other clubs were shocked."

The Zealots wear their signature Viking helmets at the 2013 National Homebrewers Conference. *Jon Airheart.*

But the Zealots' newfound success did not end there.

"We were the nobody club," Pam said. "They thought it was a fluke the first time, but then, we won again the next year."

It wasn't just the club as a whole that triumphed at the 2011 circuit but also the individual members—such as Mark Schoppe, who won the individual award, and the Bradleys, who took home the team award—making it a clean sweep for the Zealots across all three divisions.

In addition to standard homebrewing competition wins, the Bradleys have won several pro-am awards, affording them the opportunity to have their recipes brewed at craft breweries all over the country, including Ska, Funkwerks, Elliot Bay, Equinox, Uncle Billy's Brew and Que and Lagunitas.

"Lagunitas decided that they wanted to have a beer that they brewed especially for South by Southwest, so they contacted the homebrew clubs in the area, and every homebrew club had a little mini competition within its club to select the members' favorite beers to enter in the Lagunitas competition," Pam said.

Keith's beer was selected as the Carboys' entrant and sent in alongside Dan Ironside from the Zealots' entry. Both beers were sent out for judging, and Keith's beer was selected. As his prize, Keith went out to Lagunitas in January 2013 to brew the SXSW beer. He was joined by Texas Carboys founder Bob Kapusinski, who was randomly drawn to attend, Mike Baldwin from Zax Restaurant and Josh Wilson from the Draught House Pub, who both were randomly selected among retailers carrying Lagunitas in Austin. When the group bumped up to brewing Keith's beer on the much larger Lagunitas system, they tweaked the recipe a bit and ended up with a 7.1 percent intensely dry-hopped IPA with a strong malt backbone. Containing West Coast hops and East Coast malts, the beer was known as Fusion XII.

REPRESENTING THE LONE STAR STATE

Mark Schoppe brought home the Ninkasi Award at the National Homebrewers Conference in Seattle in June 2012. *Dan Dewberry.*

Competitive homebrewing isn't exactly a blood sport, but for Zealot Mark Schoppe, it does require a kind of religious dedication. He's proven himself to be a national contender with back-to-back individual Lonestar Circuit titles for 2011 and 2012, plus the 2012 National Homebrewers Conference Ninkasi Award, the most coveted award in American homebrewing. But it's not just a love for competition that drives this bearded brewer to be so, um, zealous.

"I can be very competitive, but also a bit obsessive-compulsive," Schoppe said.

After a career counselor turned him onto to the hobby during his final semester at Rice University, Schoppe began homebrewing and never looked back. He spent a summer as an assistant brewer at Saint Arnold back in 1995 but, ultimately, had to return to Austin to finish graduate school (#BestSummerVacationEver), after which he began working in the software industry. Schoppe competed in some competitions throughout the '90s but really stepped up his entries in 2008 or so, when he got inspired to do his part in helping the Austin Zealots win the Lonestar Circuit. Homebrew competitions typically have a wealth of different beer style categories, and some place a limit on the number of beers an individual club member can enter, though others do not.

"Once I passed the mental hurdle of, 'Hey, I can enter thirty beers [into a particular competition] if I really want to,' it's like, "Well how many can I enter? Can I enter forty? Can I enter fifty? Can I enter sixty?" Schoppe said. "So the most I've ever entered is seventy-six."

To brew that many different beers, Schoppe brews frequently and sticks to smaller batches.

"I tend to go in runs where I'm brewing every weekend, and I do a lot of small batches—so like a gallon and a half. And I can do three or four batches in one day," He said. "So it gives me more entries. When I first started entering a lot of beers, I was making five-gallon batches. I had so much leftover beer that it was getting too old to enter it in competitions and it was getting too old to drink it. I started doing smaller batches so I'd run out right after I got to the last competition."

While it's easy to get competitive, entering competitions can get expensive. Between entry fees and shipping costs, it is not uncommon to spend several hundred, if not several thousand, dollars a year entering beers in competitions, especially if the brewer is trying to submit beers into as many categories as possible.

"I haven't calculated how much money I've spent entering competitions, but it's a ridiculous amount," Schoppe said. "It's thousands and thousands of dollars. The NHC entry fee last year was like twelve dollars per entry, and I had sixty-two entries. And that's just entries; shipping was on top of that. And I'm entering sixty or so per competition like five or six times a year. The prizes don't come close to covering that."

Without the lure of large cash prizes (it's actually illegal to receive cash prizes in homebrew competitions in Texas), competitions will reward winners with medals, ribbons and commemorative prizes, such as beer steins, homebrew equipment and brewery merchandise. Schoppe does it all for the love of homebrewing, the thrill of competition and, recently, to persevere in a friendly rivalry he has going against Bay Area Mashtronauts member, and previous Lonestar Circuit individual title holder, Jeff Oberlin.

After three straight years of Oberlin winning the circuit, Schoppe was on a mission to beat him.

"I started in January, and I was brewing every weekend and building up a stock of beers to enter. And then, I come to find out that he decided basically to retire from the circuit," Schoppe said. "So I was all geared up to compete against him and try to beat him. And he retires. So I've won two years in a row, so I was kind of dialing it back a bit [this year] because it takes a lot of time and effort to brew these beers. So I didn't enter as much, but this year, it turns out Jeff Oberlin has decided he wants to win it again."

As a result, Oberlin destroyed Schoppe at the Alamo City Cerveza Fest, where he took home thirty-seven points against Schoppe's six. The blow just made Schoppe more determined than ever.

"The next competition in a couple weeks [July 2013] is his homebrew club's competition down in Clear Lake," Schoppe said. "They have a limit of fifty-six beers; it's the most you can enter. I'm entering fifty-six beers. I'm going all in; I'm coming after him. All I can do is hope that he's taking it easy and coasting because he's got such a big lead."

These competitive homebrewers aren't the only Austinites to be making a splash on the national stage. As a prolific member of the Austin beer community, avid homebrewer (and author of the foreword of this book) Debbie Cerda currently sits on the governing committee for the American Homebrewers Association (AHA). Elected in 2012, Cerda is currently the only Texan and one of only three women on the eighteen-person committee.

Cerda was inspired to run for the governing committee after attending the National Homebrewers Conference in Oakland in 2009. The first night of the conference, though she was excited to be there, she got a bit discouraged by the culture of the event. She witnessed a lot of fanboy idolization of prestigious male homebrewers in the room and felt as if many similarly accomplished female homebrewers were treated as little more than brewers' wives. But later that night, she met Denise Jones, brewmaster for Moylan's Brewery in Novato, California. At the same conference, she met the organizers of Queen of Beer, an all-female homebrewing competition that takes place in Placerville, California. Her conversations with these remarkable women made her feel empowered as a homebrewer. During the same conference, Cerda attended an AHA members meeting, where she interacted with members of the AHA Governing Committee. Cerda paid close attention to the discussion and asked a lot of questions. Afterward, she went up to meet some of the members of the committee. Impressed by her engagement in the discussion, some of them suggested that she herself run for a seat on the committee.

"Getting to the National Homebrewers Conference was a great opportunity to expand my world and have more confidence in myself as a brewer," Cerda said.

It is very rare for a candidate to get elected her first time running, but Cerda succeeded.

"I owe that to the support of the Texas homebrewing community," she said. "I owe that to the support of the Lonestar Circuit."

THE TEXAS CARBOYS

Started in 2009 when Bob Kapusinski put up a notice at the Dig Pub in Cedar Park for a meeting of local homebrewers, the Texas Carboys have become another formidable Austin-area homebrew club. In the beginning, ten people or so attended the meetings there at the Dig. Now, the club has forty to fifty members. While some of the Carboys reside in Austin, the club also boasts a lot of membership from the city's northern suburbs, such as Cedar Park, Leander, Round Rock and even as far north as Georgetown. The members' professions are as varied as the suburbs they hail from, with members holding down day jobs that range from mechanics to pharmacists to IT professionals to lawyers. Kapusinski remained president of the club until 2013, when Joe White took over leadership. While the club is certainly growing, the goal is for it to maintain its intimate, approachable feel.

"I want the club to remain a friendly club that welcomes new brewers and encourages learning new techniques to make better beer," White said. "The club really has become a circle of friends for me, and I want it to stay that way."

Their meetings tend to be a bit more organized than the free-for-all nature of the Austin Zealots meetings. Members sign in their homebrews on a sheet upon entering the meeting, and then, the club organizes everything into a proper tasting order, complete with a projection of the list. It gets a bit crazy after thirty beers or so, but they try to keep things in order.

In addition to their monthly meetings, the club hosts two club picnics every year at a local park, one in the spring and one in the fall. Several members of the club will volunteer to do what is known as a "brew-in," for which they all team up to brew the beer for the party. The club also hosts organized brewery tours and pub-crawls.

Though the club is relatively new compared to more seasoned clubs, such as the Austin Zealots and the Houston Foam Rangers, individual members of the Carboys have racked up medals in a number of homebrewing competitions, including the Bluebonnet Brew-Off, San Antonio's Alamo City Cerveza Fest and the Celtic Brew-Off in Arlington. Some members of the Carboys attribute their successes in statewide competitions to the skills honed from the wealth of competitions they hold within their own club each year. They've done competitions where each member of the club brews the same Austin Homebrew Supply recipe. They have also hosted inner club pro-am and am-pro competitions, in which some of the more experienced Carboys are paired up with beginners from the club. During the pro-am portion of the competition, they brew on the pro's system, and during the am-pro portion, they brew on the amateur homebrewer's introductory homebrewing kit. Next on the Carboys' agenda is an Iron Brewer competition, in which brewers will all have to brew with a secret ingredient, a la *Iron Chef*. After honing their chops in the inner-club competitions, the Carboys have moved up to sponsoring its own open tournament, the Dig Pub's Monster Homebrew competition. Held each fall, the 2012 competition only had three categories—malt monster, hop monster and otherworldly (for beers that did not quite fit within either category)—leaving entries open to broad interpretation and bold experimentation.

"I am not a very creative or 'artsy' person," White said. "Homebrewing is a chance for me to be creative. Plus, the beer is good, as is the community."

To keep fostering this growing community centered on the world's most widely consumed beverage, White has some advice to new homebrewers: "Go brew with someone else, actually, many other people. Find your own style using what you learn. And, most of all, don't worry. Relax, have a homebrew. It's more than a catchy phrase; at the end of the day, what you just brewed will be beer."

CHAPTER FIVE
A SECOND WIND

PAIRS WITH (512) PECAN PORTER

The year 2000 was upon us. We'd partied like it was 1999, survived the new millennium (big surprise, computers didn't freak out, forget whom they served or usurp the government) and discovered that we'd never really lived before we could carry every song we'd stolen off the Internet on an iPod. Powerhouse Austin craft breweries such as Real Ale and Live Oak were still blazing a trail for themselves, overcoming hurdle after hurdle. Their efforts were inadvertently reshaping the community around them, prepping it for the vast wave of breweries that began opening at the close of the decade and haven't shown any sign of slowing. Each new brewery had a distinct philosophy and perspective to bring to Austin and has continued to open up new avenues for brew-lovers across the ATX.

INDEPENDENCE BREWING COMPANY

In the late '90s, the Austin craft beer market was wide open. There were breweries beginning to bloom, such as Real Ale and Live Oak, and a couple brewpubs still letting the taps run. It wasn't long before other brew fanatics were looking for a space at the bar as well. Amy and Rob Cartwright led the stampede in the early 2000s when they began their efforts to open Independence Brewing Company.

Amy and Rob broke into brewing in the Austin brewpubs of the mid-1990s while both attended the University of Texas (UT). Rob started homebrewing in college with guys in his dorm. His mom had taught him the art of brewing, and after a rebellious stint making wine during high school (it was the early '90s grunge generation, after all), Rob embraced his inner brewer. When brewpub laws changed, Rob changed his major at UT and decided then and there that he wanted to brew for a living. He then started working at the Copper Tank under Davis Tucker. Amy, on the other hand, saw the sales side of the brew life while she was working as a hostess at the Bitter End under Tim Schwartz—yeah, Real Ale Tim Schwartz. The hostess stand at the Bitter End was situated right next to the mash tun and kettle. So to keep hungry patrons from walking out, Amy would describe the brewing process that was happening on the other side of the glass by giving tours.

After college, in 2000, the pair met. As their relationship grew, they started having conversations about starting their own brewery. By 2003, they were well on their way to opening its doors. However, there were several hardships they had to overcome.

At that time, the brewpubs in Austin were really struggling to make it, due in part to the beer laws in the city. Texas brewpubs weren't permitted to distribute their beers to other retailers, making it very difficult to evolve into a larger-scale brewing operation. Similarly, breweries weren't permitted to sell their beer on premises. Many brewpubs, including Waterloo and the Copper Tank, shut their doors in the early 2000s as a testament to how difficult it had become to make it. The Bitter End, of course, caught fire in 2005 and was never reopened. The breweries that were around in Austin, namely Real Ale and Live Oak, were becoming large operations, but both had fought hard for their spots in the market. There were other breweries in Texas—such as Saint Arnold in Houston and, of course, Shiner—but not many. People weren't willing to invest in a wild idea like a new brewery, so the couple had trouble raising sufficient funds to cover all the costs of starting up a brewery.

"[For] breweries now, because it's a proven investment, it's been easier for people to raise money," Amy said.

Amy and Rob took on a do-it-yourself mentality because they didn't have this big war chest to draw from. By 2004, they'd found a warehouse space on the south side of town and started up their operation. They had an old, small system from the '80s that they'd gotten a deal on. From there, they spent the next few months building the rest of the brewery by hand, from

Independence Brewing cofounder Amy Cartwright dresses up as Elvis during a First Saturday tour in January 2005 in which the brewery celebrated the King's birthday. *Amy Cartwright.*

the cold room to the mill. By October, they were brewing their first three beers. As Texas brewers weren't allowed to sell their wares on the premises, there was no way to make immediate revenue through taste tests of smaller batches. So they found they needed to jump in feet first. To mitigate some of the risk, they strove to fill a hole in the craft market. They came to market with beers such as Austin Amber and Bootlegger Brown to satiate the need for local amber and brown ales in Austin.

Keep in mind, though, folks, that in 2004, people weren't retweeting 24/7 or obsessing over their Facebook feed or checking their Reddit every morning over coffee. The best you could hope for in the way of social media was your junior high crush reading a heartfelt (i.e., teenage angst–fueled) confession on your Xanga journal. Amy had to hit the street old school to sell Independence beers to the community.

"Pretty much I was doing all of our sales and delivery," Amy said. "Getting the word out was a lot harder back then."

To get their foot in the door with local bars, they would send out letters and host parties so employees could experience the beers. Amy would drive the trucks, haul kegs into establishments around town and then introduce herself to the patrons on the other side of the bar and invite them out to the brewery, making her an incontestably badass lady of brew.

Despite Amy's gung-ho approach and Rob's solid line of beers, making a name for themselves wasn't proving easy at the turn of the millennium. Bars around Austin didn't have the behemoth tap walls that they do now.

"Dog & Duck has almost doubled the size of its tap wall since we started," Amy said. "It was unheard of for a place like Banger's to have one hundred taps."

Moreover, the macrobrewed beers tied up a large proportion of the taps that were available. Add to that local competitors—such as Real Ale, with its renowned Firemans #4 and Rio Blanco Pale, and Live Oak, which also has an exceptionally solid beer lineup with its HefeWeizen—and it was damn near impossible to catch people's eyes. That is what drew Independence to brown ales. Its biggest competition doing brown ale at the time was Newcastle, so being a local, young brewery gave it a foot up in that respect. Soon, its beer started drawing a loyal following. After about a year of Rob and Amy running the shop just the two of them, they opened their bottling line, brought on a crew and took their business to a whole new level.

"It was a whole different experience getting into grocery stores," Amy said.

It had a solid foothold in the bars with its beers on tap, but getting product on the shelves in the area was a huge leap forward for Independence. By 2008, the team was in a really solid place. It started developing more progressive beers, such as Convict Hill Oatmeal Stout and Stash IPA.

By then, Amy and Rob had a crew and a company to run. They went from building the brewery to handling human resources issues and managing payroll. It was a challenge moving into managerial roles, but it prepared them for the growth they would soon see.

By the brewery's fifth anniversary, Rob and Amy were ready to focus on starting their family together. Once the couple got pregnant, Amy clearly couldn't be carrying kegs around town. They started getting their beer out through Brown Distributing shortly thereafter. Unsurprisingly, with that came a new batch of challenges.

"When you make a move from self-distributing to working with a distributer, they have to make their cut somehow," she said.

Rather than all of a sudden raising prices for the consumers, however, Independence pushed to produce and sell more beer to balance out during the transition. In 2010, Independence was expanding fast, adding more fermenters and buying $75,000 worth of kegs. Through this huge push, it essentially reinvented all of its processes and nearly quadrupled its volume.

The Alamo Drafthouse screens a showing of *Strange Brew* at Independence Brewing headquarters as part of its Rolling Roadshow Series. *Amy Cartwright.*

"[We were] moving from brewing once a day to three times a day," Amy said.

When newer breweries, such as (512), came on the scene in Austin, Independence was introduced to a sense of friendly competition that pushed them to do more creative beers, such as its Brewluminati series, which are all single-batch and draft-only brews. These run the gambit from Brouwer's Dubbel to Citrification American IPA to Humbucker Belgian Pale Ale and Working Dog Winter Warmer with a variety of still more styles in between. Independence continues to chug out interesting and sought-after beers. Independence's mainstays, though—such as its grapefruity Stash IPA and its crisp, clean Independence Pale Ale—keep newbie breweries aware of the quality available in market that they need to meet.

After over a decade of forging its way into the craft beer market, Independence is one of the largest local breweries Austin has to offer. Today, it produces six year-round selections, including Austin Amber, Bootlegger Brown, Freestyle Wheat and Convict Hill Oatmeal Stout, as well as a handful of rotating seasonals and the aforementioned experimental single-batch brews that aim to push the envelope on creativity. In addition, the brewery has become an icon in Austin and the Texas Hill Country.

BLACK STAR CO-OP

At the close of 2005, after traveling for some time in Belgium, Steven Yarak, a young professional, came to the conclusion that he wanted to start a community-owned pub like those he visited abroad with a special Texas flair. He began the pursuit for a group of people who could make his dream a reality. Sixteen people attended the first co-op meeting in January 2006, including Jeff Young, a young man fresh out of the American Brewers' Guild's Intensive Brewing Science & Engineering (IBS&E) program and recovering from being pretty beaten down by life.

Young had been working in Alabama at a mining facility called Chemical Lime for a little over a year while also trying to earn his degree in chemistry. This was not his first stint at Chemical Lime, having worked as a chemist while he studied mathematics and electrical engineering some time before, but after a disastrous and short-lived move to Austin to attend UT, he returned home to reevaluate his direction in life. Young had a variety of passions and interests that seemed constantly at odds with each other. He had a deep foundation in mathematics and the sciences but also had an appreciation for art history, a love of philosophy and a creative energy that were being sorely repressed. His second tour with Chemical Lime ended up making him more miserable, though. With his coursework, he would stay awake working and studying for forty-eight hours at a time twice a week. He was crying his sorrows into pint after pint of ice cream on his one day off a week. Well, maybe not crying his sorrows, but there were definitely many, many pints of ice cream—until he found brewing.

Brewing beer was the ultimate synergy of all the things he passionately wanted to pursue. He could utilize his extensive chemistry and engineering background while creating something organic and dynamic and name it after cool math terms. Unwilling to lose any more time, he enrolled with the American Brewers' Guild and set out on changing his life.

After a couple interviews with breweries across the country that were "just not the right fit" for him, Young returned to Austin, where one can only guess he planned to reappropriate the horribly traumatic memories

Jeff Young earns his keep at Black Star Co-op. *Suzy Schaffer.*

he held from his short time at UT. Less than a week after arriving, he was invited to Black Star's first meeting. It was there he presented a momentous proposition: If a cooperative pub would be cool, wouldn't a cooperative brewpub be even cooler?

However, making the brewpub come together in a co-op environment was anything but easy. The group was hugely interested in collaboration and blending concepts but lacked direction and straightforwardness in the approach of collecting those concepts. The process of defining what the co-op would be and what fundamental ideals it would stand for stretched on for nearly three years. It boiled down to another set of contradicting forces. Starting a business requires a clear vision. Without that, any cool "what if we do this" idea runs the risk of convoluting, if not completely derailing, the project. Still, the growing member-owners of Black Star co-op pushed forward and began collecting funds. By 2010, they had raised more than $325,000, found a location that could accommodate the brewpub and replaced a lot of the idealism with a realistic vision. About a year after they opened, the co-op board members agreed on a system of rules to govern the business and the day-to-day workings that made it a success. These rules are constantly in a state of evolution because, as with any system of rules, they cannot be "both consistent and complete." However, this openness to innovative thought and collaborative concepts was nothing new to the team at Black Star. Based off the seven principles cooperatives use and customized to suit this one-of-a-kind project, the chaos of having too many voices died down, and the co-op began to thrive.

During this time, Young was hard at work gathering collaborators of his own. Part of his vision for brewing was involving the community. As when a party of people goes to a restaurant and enjoys a meal that was prepared moments before by a chef it can engage, Young wanted his patrons to have that access to him as they enjoyed the beers he had brewed, and moreover, he wanted them to participate in what was coming next. His tactical strategy was to divide Black Star's portfolio into two types of beers: rationals and irrationals.

These terms are derived from his background in mathematics. A balanced number line is composed of two types of numbers: rational numbers and irrational ones. A rational number can be derived from a variety of equations and can be represented as a ratio. The number four is rational because it can be represented as four divided by one. Irrational numbers cannot be represented as a ratio. An example would be the number pi. One could not represent pi as a fraction. It's a nonrepeating integer that goes on into infinity. But a number line needs pi and other irrational numbers to balance out all the rationals.

So Young, with the input of countless beer lovers, set out to create a collection of balanced beers that were approachable and drinkable but that would also wow serious beer connoisseurs with their crafted nuances. These would be his rationals.

"These are the beers that keep [Black Star's] door open," Young said.

One of the greatest moments of collaboration for the brewpub came from the development of these rational beers. Young put out a competition for member-owners to submit American wheat ale recipes, expecting to put it out for a short time as an irrational collaboration beer. What actually was born of that, though, was Elba, one of the co-op's most successful beers and a mainstay on the rational docket.

Young's irrational brews are, for the most part, hugely experimental. They are the edgy daredevils of the brewpub. The flavors aren't always for everyone, but the innovative thought behind them is, nonetheless, pretty impressive. From fermenting with fresh black truffles to aging in Brimstone whiskey barrels, Young lets his creativity loose and goes to great lengths to capture the specific profiles he is looking for in his concepts. He traveled to Scotland to collect peat-smoked oak barrels for his Infinite series, though he ended up trading the Scottish barrels out for Balcones Brimstone barrels treated in a one-of-a-kind oak-smoked process up the road in Waco.

"The irrationals keep [new] people coming through the door," he said.

Canning, bottling and kegging might be in the future for Young and the team at Black Star, as well as coordinating with a distribution partner to get beers into choice establishments around the city. All this very well might be part of a carefully calculated scheme to promote a yet undisclosed second location on the southeastern side of Austin. Anywhere we can find the tasty, brainy and balanced libations is a rational choice for us.

(512) Brewing Company

There are few things as iconic to Austin as the numbers 512, the original area code for local phone numbers (now there's also 737, which, let's face it, doesn't quite have the same level of history or cool behind it). When Kevin Brand was a kid growing up in San Antonio, the (512) extended all across the Hill Country, and it has always resonated with him. After falling in love with beer in 1992 while working at a local beer store, he spent many years homebrewing, eventually moving out West and brewing in California while working in medical device development. It got to the point that he was brewing more than he could drink and was feeling a little burned out from the daily grind, not to mention more than a bit homesick for the Hill Country, so he packed back up and headed home. It took a little more encouragement from his family, but in 2007, Brand made the jump and took the first steps to opening (512) Brewing Company.

The breweries that were already established were very welcoming to Brand.

"It was great," Brand said. "It was a lot of fun to meet a small amount of people, and getting to know just a few breweries was pretty easy. It was one of the reasons I got into this, the people I met here specifically."

Brand spent a lot of time going on brewery tours, particularly those at Live Oak Brewing. Chip McElroy realized that he was there quite a bit and asked what Brand wanted to do with all the information he was amassing. Chip, as well as team members from Real Ale and Independence, was all very willing to share their experiences with opening a brewery.

"It was really cool to come on the scene with only a few other breweries in the area," said Brand. "Their willingness to share was so appealing and not typical for other industries."

Brand modeled his business after how Live Oak Brewing was running things. He liked the idea of draft only and growing slowly. Brand, who's a big proponent of sourcing ingredients as close to the brewery as possible and working to get as many organic ingredients into the beer as possible—it's a little known fact that at least 80 percent of every beer (512) produces is organic—wanted to brew beers that embodied Americanized English- and Belgian-style beers that were new and creative. He wanted to do beer styles that he loved and that were underrepresented at the time, taking on creative takes of IPAs and pale ales. A big influence for Brand was Celis Brewery, which inspired beers such as the (512) Wit. Overall, he wanted to blend in with the other styles in this area without necessarily going head to head with them. He wanted to add variety for people who were looking for it around town.

This idea of being part of the community and representative of it is embodied in the name (512). It's a name about the collective.

"It's a way of saying Austin without saying Austin. It was nice that it included so many different areas. It's neat to see other people refer to Austin in (512) terms," Brand said.

Getting the brewery up and running was a pretty seamless transition for Brand and his crew. It was a wild idea that Brand could start up his own business in an industry he was not familiar with at all, really. He made a deal with himself that he would get the things he thought were necessary all lined up, and if any of them were insurmountable, he'd go back to his other career. Then, when it came to learning how to run the brewery and the business at that level, nothing came up as insurmountable. So he kept going.

The cash wasn't holding him back, and the wheels were turning. In five years, (512) has grown from 1,200 barrels to nearly 10,000 barrels in 2013 alone.

The market is vast, and Brand has a knack for encouraging people to try new beers.

"Even if they don't like one of our styles, I can usually convince them to try something else from one of these local breweries that might convert them for life to drinking these handmade beers," Brand said.

However, it would be tough to dislike all the styles of beer (512) is producing. They have five year-round styles, including the legendary (512) Pecan Porter.

A pumpkin at the October 2012 Texas Craft Brewers Festival is emblazoned with the (512) logo. *Holly Aker.*

(512) Brewing Company facilities stand behind the pecan tree that inspired its famous (512) Pecan Porter. *Sarah Wood.*

"It's probably the one most people identify with us," Brand said.

Brand wanted something darker in his portfolio and, one day, saw the pecan tree outside the brewery and thought it would be a good mix. Pecans are something people identify with Austin and the Hill Country, and the Pecan Porter became something (512) started continuously brewing right away. It's dark and roasted and nutty, but in a really subtle way. (It's also the companion beer to this chapter, so perhaps you're enjoying one now.) The (512) IPA is a balanced, malty, bold, hoppy beer with a lot of Glacier and Simcoe hops that make the beer mild and midrange from the bitterness standpoint. It's a little grapefruity and floral but, overall, is maltier than most IPAs.

Outside its core beers, (512) has a line of seasonals that are very quick to go when they are released on the market. These include the killer Whiskey Barrel Aged Double Pecan Porter, which, aside from being a mouthful in more than one way, is very near and dear to Brand's heart.

"It's one of the beers I love to drink; people get excited for it; and it certainly creates a big buzz around the brewery when we brew it," said Brand.

To make the beer, (512) brews a double batch of Pecan Porter and ages it in Jack Daniel's Whiskey barrels. The result is a really dark, almost coffee-like, bitterness that takes on the whiskey flavor and even some of the oak of the barrel. The other seasonals, like their anniversary ales, also make a huge splash in the community when they are released.

"We like to be thought of as food-related brewing," Brand said. "One of our key differentiators in the marketplace is our integration of some key food ingredients. The creative side of the business is what keeps people energized about being here."

(512) has become one of the larger breweries in the area and has seen huge success while still cohesively blending into the community. It is focusing on optimizing its space while also looking toward its cask program and several barrel-aged beers that it is planning to release in 2013.

"We are going to continue to crank out new creations," said Brand. "We want to be the kind of brewery that people feel like they know well and can rely on at the bar as a staple. We are committed to organic grain and domestic ingredients and local stuff, and we are committed to this area."

UNCLE BILLY'S BREW AND QUE

Uncle Billy's Brew and Que is a popular brewpub situated walking distance from Zilker Park and Barton Springs pool. It is named after William "Uncle Billy" Barton, an early settler of Stephen F. Austin's second colony who, in 1837, patented and settled on the land near Barton Springs. He promoted the springs far and wide and is credited with the popularity surrounding it throughout the 180 years that have since elapsed, although, admittedly, his presence in the twittersphere has decreased in recent years.

Uncle Billy's Brew and Que opened in 2007, and from the get-go, the philosophy behind the venture was centered on taking as much time and care with the beers they were brewing as they did the barbecue they were smoking and keeping everything consistent and as good as it ever was. A second location that boasted the brew and the cue with a view, plus a slew of musical crews (#RockAMicLikeAVandal), was opened in 2010 on Lake Travis. Unfortunately, the Lake Travis location closed in the fall of 2012 due to a venue that was pricey to keep up with and a record-breaking drought that kept the crowds off the lake through the summer. However, the original Barton Springs location has stood the test of time.

The brewing operation was originally led by the legendary Brian "Swifty" Peters, who was fundamental in brewing at places like the Bitter End and Live Oak Brewing. In 2010, Amos Lowe joined the brew crew, and through the years, Uncle Billy's beers, such as the Bottle Rocket Lager and the Hell in Keller Keller Bier, have won several medals at the Great American Beer Festival and even a bronze medal at the 2010 World Beer Cup. The pair had a solid following but wanted to move on to other ventures. However, the two needed to pass their legacy at Uncle Billy's to someone who shared their perspective on beer. Michael Waters was waiting patiently for them to pass the torch his way.

Waters, a native of Florida, began homebrewing when he moved to San Antonio.

"That really opened my palate up to craft beer," Waters said.

He was introduced to Peters and Justin Rizza of Independence and Flix Brewhouse during this time and really respected both of them. Fundamentally, they all shared common principles about brewing, and under their careful mentorship shaping his homebrew endeavors, Waters built a very strong foundation in brewing.

From the time Uncle Billy's opened in 2007, it was a paramount stop whenever Waters was in Austin—so much so, in fact, that in 2009, he

Former Uncle Billy's brewer Brian "Swifty" Peters shows off his GABF gold medal for Bottle Rocket. *Holly Aker.*

moved from San Antonio to Austin. He began volunteering at Independence Brewing shortly thereafter on the bottling line, and within six months, he was brewing next to Rizza. When Rizza left Independence, Waters stepped up into the head brewer position, heading up production at a pivotal time in the brewery's history. However, when Peters and Lowe suggested that he should take over brewing operations over at the remaining Uncle Billy's, he had to take them up on their offer.

Waters had a love for many of the qualities Lowe and Peters aimed for in their beers. They wanted to brew technically sound beers and had a history of consistently great award-winning beers to pass on.

"You don't have to follow traditions, but there are things that universally make great beers," Waters said.

The three gentlemen also all had a love of dry, clean, bright ales and lagers, which are a mainstay on the menu at Uncle Billy's. So the transfer of knowledge and eventual transfer of power began. Peters and Lowe stayed on with Waters for a few months to acclimate him to the system and the difference in production. It was a little difficult for Waters coming from a production brewery into a brewpub atmosphere, but overall, it was a pretty seamless transition, due largely to the existing friendships and similarities in brewing philosophies.

After a few months, Peters and Lowe stepped back, and Waters began taking off as the head brewer. He kept many of the original recipes on tap, tweaking them here and there. With the growth the craft market has seen in Austin over the years, he found it important to keep that market satiated with aggressive and sophisticated beers that are solidly brewed. He didn't look for things that were interesting for interesting's sake. Most importantly, he brewed things he loved to drink.

The entrance to Uncle Billy's Brew and Que off Barton Springs Road welcomes thirsty guests. *Sarah Wood.*

"The South Austin [community] loves its IPAs," Waters said.

Waters is very accommodating with that. He beefed up the Axe Handle with extra hops and also started brewing IPAs, such as the Green Room, which is fruity, crisp and bright with a killer floral nose, serving them up next to other representatives of the style, such as Hop Zombie, which is piney while still being really citrusy. To balance things out, Waters stocks the bar with darker beers, including the dry stout the Mo'Connor and the Hill Country Amber. He stocks growlers and is currently looking into producing cans and kegs that brew fanatics can take away from the brewpub.

Uncle Billy's location gives the brewpub a lot of visibility in the community. "It's a nice place to be with interesting people," Michael said.

There is a group of regulars that man the bar almost every day, but also, a constant flow of new faces stops in to try a brew after a day at Barton Springs or an evening at Blues on the Green or Austin City Limits Festival. This constant influx of new and old beer drinkers keeps the atmosphere dynamic while Waters strives to maintain a consistent experience with the brew. Uncle Billy's aims to be a great option for fresh, well-crafted artisan beer that is consistent and thoughtful. They take things slowly at Uncle Billy's, make changes gradually and are rewarded with happy beer lovers from all over Austin.

Adelbert's Brewery

Near the end of the decade, the beer community welcomed in several breweries, including Adelbert's, a brewery focused on Belgian-style ales situated in the north side of the city. Adelbert's Brewery is the brainchild of Scott Hovey and Greg Smith, a couple of Austin-based electrical engineers. It is named after Hovey's older brother, George Adelbert Hovey, known as Del to his friends and family, who passed away in 2000.

"Del introduced [Scott] to craft beer," Billy Murff of Adelbert's said.

Del was an adventurer and quite the storyteller. Hovey wanted to commemorate his brother and the stories he left behind, and the beer that he loved was a near-perfect vehicle on which that legacy could be carried.

With the concept and the heart of the operation set, Hovey began work on the beers he'd bring to market. He had a particular love for Belgian-style ales and a drive for perfecting age-old Belgian techniques.

"We brew Belgians because Scott likes Belgians," Murff said. "That's the beer he likes to drink, so that's the beer he wanted to brew."

Luckily, he also had an Austin market that had a deficiency in Belgian-style breweries. Belgians ales are top-fermenting, often bottle-conditioned beers that have a malty fruitiness but also a complexity and depth that comes from the natural carbonation process that takes place with bottle conditioning. The extra steps of bottle conditioning add about another three weeks to the fermentation time of the beer. During that period, it has to be very carefully monitored to ensure the flavors stay on track and the carbonation process is taking place. To make Adelbert's especially authentic, Hovey used only Bohemian hops and malt imported from the Czech Republic and Germany. The end result of these precautions is a high-end beer that is balanced and drinkable while still being very complex.

Being both sessionable and sophisticated makes Belgians excellent for pairing with food. Think of them as the girl you take home to mom. She's smart and pretty and damn well needs to know how to cook if she's going to marry anyone who is worth a thing in this world. OK, Belgians aren't that girl, but they are your cool friend who's deep and thoughtful but super easygoing. Anything from

Adelbert's head brewer and coowner Scott Hovey gives a tour of the brewery. *Holly Aker.*

The Adelbert's moniker proudly hangs outside the brewery doors. *Holly Aker.*

a plate of grilled chicken and seasoned vegetables to rich chocolate desserts to spicy dishes benefits from a great Belgian. The flavors stand up in depth while not crossing the line into overpowering the flavors of the meal.

Apart from the styles of beer, Adelbert's Brewery's beginnings were also different from other breweries in the area in that it started bottling and distributing around the state immediately after opening its doors. Because of the substantial initial costs of bottling and the typically unstable starts breweries experience—it takes a couple revs to get the recipes right more often than not—it's tough for a company to take the proverbial leap and ante up to the bottling line. Hovey and Smith saw the value, however, in having a bottle with their marketing and their message that they could send out across the state.

"Coming to market without a small package makes your life much harder," Murff said. "You don't get the brand recognition and your name out there. [Bottling] opens a whole market that doesn't want to spend all its time in a bar."

There is value in having an image that almost every person who drinks your product can remember, and breweries don't always get that value when their customers interact with a blank pint glass filled with delicious craft on draft. Smith and Hovey also saw the value in reaching the customer and building those connections through self-distribution.

"It was a conscious effort to get our face and our name out to other cities to grow all of the markets," Murff said.

Even with the success and growth it has experienced since opening, Adelbert's continues to self-distribute as a means to stay connected with its consumers and clients. It gets live feedback from all its patrons, which has helped shape Adelbert's lineup.

However, formulating the process to distribute for itself was by no means all pie and punch and actually ended up being more of a challenge than the team had initially thought.

"The biggest hardships were organizing the distribution and coordinating it with the brew schedule because we were brewing nine beers at once," Murff said. "[It took time] getting the system built that worked. Every time we'd come across something, we'd have to adjust the system."

Coordinating the brew schedule with the distribution schedule is near impossible when trying to juggle brewing nine different beers at any one time. With any product, you have to get it out on time, but you also have to respect the time it takes for Belgians to come into their own in the bottle.

As it found its cadence, however, Adelbert's Brewery became a very well-received addition to the beer community in Austin as well as in Houston and Dallas.

Beer was the official publication of the Texas Brewers Institute in the late 1930s. Shortly after the repeal of Prohibition, it proclaimed beer as a "beverage of moderation." Beer *(November 1939 to September 1940). Texas Brewers Institute. Texas State Archives.*

Above: Johann "Jean" Schneider's beer vaults are now used as a private underground dining room at La Condesa. *Caroline Wallace.*

Left: Due to recent legislative changes, Jester King is now able to sell beer by the glass out of its taproom. *Holly Aker.*

Opposite: Pawnee the miniature donkey was on hand to help Pinthouse Pizza celebrate the release of its Burro's Breakfast Mexican lager. *Holly Aker.*

The Thirsty Planet crew goes apeshit in gorilla suits for a 2013 Gorilla Run event. Gorilla Run is an annual charity 5K benefiting the Mountain Gorilla Conservation Fund. *Holly Aker.*

Shotgun Friday, a holy day for craft beer lovers, is celebrated by shotgunning a can of craft beer with fellow beer enthusiasts. *Wes Kitten and the Beer Haul.*

Partygoers enjoy beers at Adelbert's grand opening party in 2012. *Holly Aker.*

A volunteer pours a beer in the Jester King taproom. *Holly Aker.*

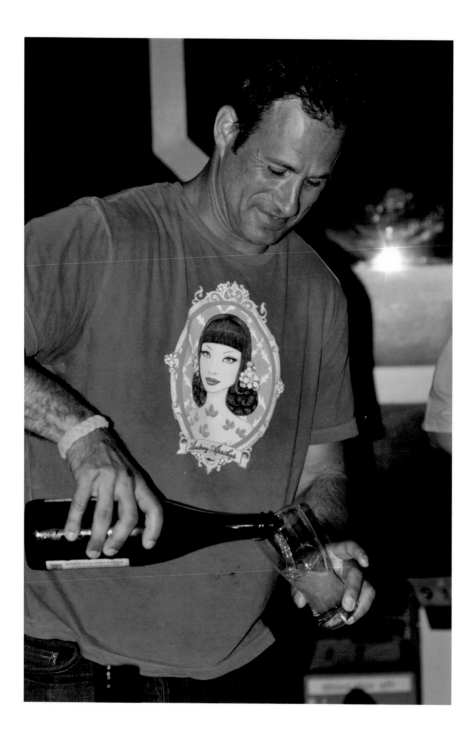

Above: Pinthouse Pizza serves up beer in a British-style pint glass. The extra volume allows for the appropriate amount of head. *Shaun Martin.*

Opposite: Dogfish Head's Sam Calagione pours beer at the Off-Centered Film Festival in Austin. *Holly Aker.*

The Hops & Grain crew changed its license from brewery to brewpub with the legislative changes in June 2013. *Kat McCullough.*

Black Star Co-op brewer Jeff Young's boots were made for co-oping. *Courtesy of Black Star Co-op.*

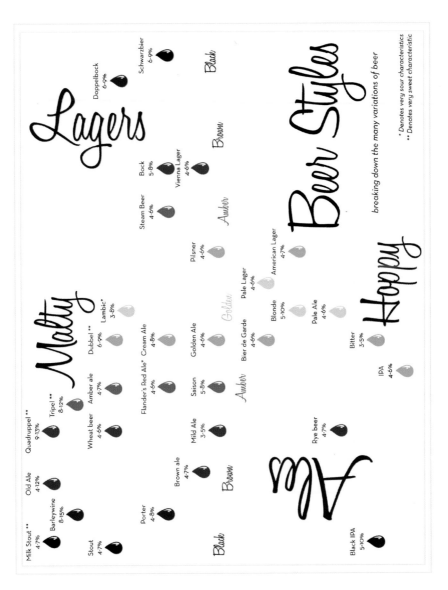

Beer styles infographic. *Sarah Wood.*

Jester King's annual Funk n' Sour festival celebrates beers that utilize wild yeast and souring bacteria. *Holly Aker.*

It's no wonder brewers call themselves "glorified janitors." Keeping tanks as shiny as this is a critical part of the brewing process. *Wes Kitten and the Beer Haul.*

Homebrewer Andrew Frazier shares one of his creations with friends at a bottle share. *Holly Aker.*

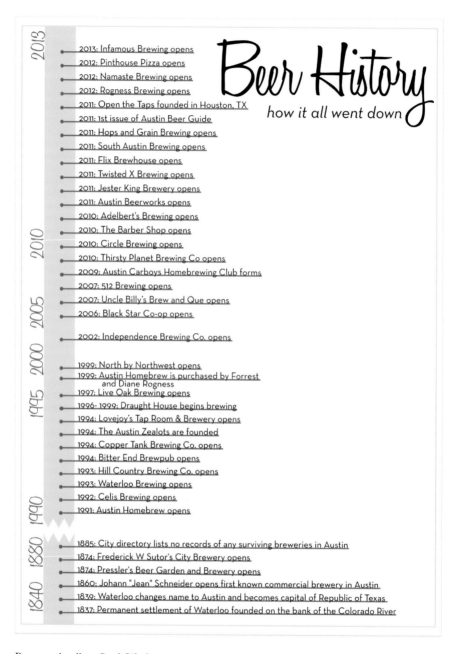

Beer History

how it all went down

- 2013: Infamous Brewing opens
- 2012: Pinthouse Pizza opens
- 2012: Namaste Brewing opens
- 2012: Rogness Brewing opens
- 2011: Open the Taps founded in Houston, TX
- 2011: 1st issue of Austin Beer Guide
- 2011: Hops and Grain Brewing opens
- 2011: South Austin Brewing opens
- 2011: Flix Brewhouse opens
- 2011: Twisted X Brewing opens
- 2011: Jester King Brewery opens
- 2011: Austin Beerworks opens
- 2010: Adelbert's Brewing opens
- 2010: The Barber Shop opens
- 2010: Circle Brewing opens
- 2010: Thirsty Planet Brewing Co opens
- 2009: Austin Carboys Homebrewing Club forms
- 2007: 512 Brewing opens
- 2007: Uncle Billy's Brew and Que opens
- 2006: Black Star Co-op opens
- 2002: Independence Brewing Co. opens
- 1999: North by Northwest opens
- 1999: Austin Homebrew is purchased by Forrest and Diane Rogness
- 1997: Live Oak Brewing opens
- 1996- 1999: Draught House begins brewing
- 1994: Lovejoy's Tap Room & Brewery opens
- 1994: The Austin Zealots are founded
- 1994: Copper Tank Brewing Co. opens
- 1994: Bitter End Brewpub opens
- 1993: Hill Country Brewing Co. opens
- 1993: Waterloo Brewing opens
- 1992: Celis Brewing opens
- 1991: Austin Homebrew opens
- 1885: City directory lists no records of any surviving breweries in Austin
- 1874: Frederick W Sutor's City Brewery opens
- 1874: Pressler's Beer Garden and Brewery opens
- 1860: Johann "Jean" Schneider opens first known commercial brewery in Austin
- 1839: Waterloo changes name to Austin and becomes capital of Republic of Texas
- 1837: Permanent settlement of Waterloo founded on the bank of the Colorado River

2013 2010 2005 2000 1995 1990 1880 1840

Brewery timeline. *Sarah Wood.*

The Beerliner, a mobile beer-dispensing bus owned by Davis Tucker, journeyed to the Great American Beer Festival to serve Texas beer samples to lucky passersby. *Holly Aker.*

Independence Brewing's business took off when it started bottling and distributing its beers in places such as Whole Foods. *Ari Auber.*

Attendee at the Texas Craft Brewers Festival represents the Lone Star State. *Holly Aker.*

Left: Austin's Mexican free-tailed bat population flies over partygoers at a Bats & Beers boat party on Lady Bird Lake. *Holly Aker.*

Below: Taps gleam in Thirsty Planet's tasting room. *Jon Airheart.*

Top: Rogness Brewing opened in 2012. *Caroline Wallace.*

Center: Tim Schwartz (left) and Brian "Swifty" Peters (right) show off their GABF medals in 2002 when both worked for the Bitter End Bistro and Brewery. They took home silvers for the Prescott's Wee Heavy and for the Lip Burner Lamb-Beak. *Kathy Towns.*

Bottom: Real Ale brewer Tim Schwartz (left) and former Uncle Billy's brewer Brian "Swifty" Peters (right) model their medals at GABF 2012. *Holly Aker.*

"All the people that work there are really great; there is never any fuss, [and] we are all on the same page. And it's beer," Murff said.

Although there were hiccups along the way getting product out, much more often than not, people enthusiastically drank and enjoyed the Belgians Smith and Hovey doled out. The community appreciated the craft taken with the beers as well as the fact that Belgians are very balanced and are unrivaled when it comes to pairing with food. When people started to understand the connections to Del and the sentimentality of each beer Hovey was producing, it added a layer of ethos to the experience of drinking Adelbert's Brewery beer.

Each beer in the Adelbert's portfolio is named after either a story Del would tell or a moniker he would go by. The Rambler blonde ale, an ester-filled, easy-drinking beer, is named after the car he drove his pals around in during the '60s, a red Rambler referred to as the "Go-Mobile." The Dancin' Monk dubbel commemorates the Colombian monks who would cut a rug like there was no tomorrow at the annual retreats Del hosted. The Philosophizer saison was a nickname for the man himself, who often imparted his words of wisdom over cold beers to those seeking counsel.

"The most interesting beer to see grow has been the Philosophizer," Murff said. "There have been a number of things that have changed and grown about it, and to see it come around to where it is now—which is pretty damn good—has been pretty cool. It's more true to the flavor of a traditional Belgian saison. It's more about dialing it in to where we wanted it to be all along."

Adelbert's Brewery has some big changes in the works, foremost among them being tentative plans to grow their vintage series, which will mean more oak barrel–aged Belgians for Austinites and out-of-towners alike to enjoy. Mostly, though, they are sticking with, at least for the present, brewing the beer they love in Del's memory and sharing those memories with a community eager to belly up to the conditioned bottles time and time again.

CIRCLE BREWING COMPANY

Ben Sabel and Judson Mulherin, founders of Circle Brewing Company, were childhood friends who grew up in Nashville, Tennessee. During their teens, they started brewing together, fermenting three-gallon batches of lagers in Sabel's mom's fridge for weeks at a time. They didn't have the recipes down right off the bat.

"Those first batches were terrible, but it was a start. I don't know if we even drank all of it, even back in high school," Sabel said.

It wasn't until seven years later that Sabel considered the idea of brewing in a professional context. He held an internship in Willsonville, Oregon, visited Oregon's Brewer's Festival and saw what a vibrant brew community was out there. It was then that he was reawakened by what craft beer could be. He reached out to Mulherin, who was in California at the time, and approached him with the idea of opening the brewery. The two started laying down plans and perfecting recipes. They also started to consider different names for the brewery. They went back and forth and around in circles on a few different options, but once Circle arose as a contender, it was tough to shake it off.

"The circle is this perfect shape. It's simplicity embodied," Sabel said.

The decision to come to Austin wasn't a difficult one for Sabel and Mulherin to make by any means. In 2007, the craft beer community was just coming into its own without having a market supersaturated with breweries. The two moved down and got jobs working in the industry. Sabel worked at Uncle Billy's Brew and Que under Brian "Swifty" Peters just after the brewpub opened, and Mulherin took a position at Independence Brewing on the bottling line working under Justin Rizza and Amy and Rob Cartwright.

The next step in the process was getting funding to open their doors. They had estimated it would take about a year to raise the money they'd need to get their operation started but did not bank on the economy becoming unstable. Raising money was a challenge. They started raising money a week or two after the financial crisis took place and continued to struggle to raise the collateral they needed for the next two and a half years.

They did raise the money, however, and in 2010, Sabel and Mulherin signed the lease on their brewing space. It took them roughly nine months to build out the brewery and get the beer making started, but in early 2011, the first kegs of Blur Texas Hefe and Envy Amber rolled out the door. One of the most rewarding moments for Sabel was walking into the Draught House after the kegs had gone out and seeing people drinking and enjoying Circle's beers.

"It was a really cool moment to look around and say, 'We did this thing, and people are enjoying something we made,'" Sabel said.

Getting the beer out the door initially didn't mark the end of their work, however, and the level of effort necessary to keep the doors open didn't wane for the two.

"It's a tough business with a lot of hard work and long hours," Sabel said.

For the first year, they were the only employees of the brewery. Mulherin would do the deliveries around town while Sabel took care of the day-to-day

Ben Sabel (left) and Judson Mulherin (right) of Circle Brewing Company pose at the Great American Beer Festival in 2012. *Caroline Wallace.*

business in the brewery. On the weekends, they would brew. After that first year, they took on one delivery driver, but it wasn't until the summer of 2013 that they started to grow their team out to six members to accommodate the new bottling line they had installed.

Circle Brewing is committed to creating the best representations possible of a particular style using only the four core ingredients of beer—hops, barley, yeast and water—in accordance with Reinheitsgebot, or the German beer purity law. Originally, this law was put in place in Germany and other areas of Bavaria partially to protect bakers from having their necessary ingredients, like rye and wheat, from being whipped up by grabby brewers. Now, it represents an ideal that beer can be excellent using only the purest of ingredients. Circle isn't trying to be a brewery that is everything for everyone, but it has a very loyal following that appreciates the pure approach it strives toward.

"We want every one of our beers to be the perfect beer of that style," Sabel. "When you are using simply those four ingredients and you focus on using just those four ingredients, it makes a really great product."

Because of this very focused stance on brewing, Sabel and Mulherin carefully analyze the development of new beers.

"It can be hard because we take styles and improvise on them a bit," Sabel said.

During development, the guys dedicate one day to brewing three five-gallon test batches. For each of the three batches, the guys change one or maybe two variables in the recipe. One batch may have slightly more hops than the others, or may have a little more malt. After the brew, they taste the batches and discern where the flavors balance out. This could take several revamps. Envy, for example, took thirty-eight different recipe trials to get spot on.

The result is exactly what they worked so hard for, though. Envy, Circle's amber, tries to be balanced in terms of bitterness and maltiness. It is full bodied and sophisticated with fruity notes. Sabel and Mulherin wanted it to be sessionable and thus worked to keep the ABV below 5.0 percent.

Other beers Circle produces include an IPA called Hop Overboard and Wryteous. Hop Overboard is a pale ale named after three Circle tanks that were lost at sea when they fell off a ship on the way to Texas. It's really floral and hoppy but rounded out with Munich and caramel malts. In the summers, the guys release Wryteous, a seasonal rye-wheat IPA that is both creamy and spicy while also maintaining a citrusy balance that makes it all-too drinkable in the summer months. Seriously, it's entirely too easy to get day drunk on this would-be sessionable beer simply because it's so delicious.

Circle began bottling in the summer of 2013. Bottling made more sense for the team. They have experience with bottling and have more control over the stability of the product. They haven't counted cans out, though.

"Our blonde in a Tallboy would be pretty cool," Sabel said.

Other plans Sabel and Mulherin have in the works include redesigning their taps. Each one is handmade by Sabel, who is very excited for the new design. That, paired with the efforts of their new marketing manager, will bring this cool brewery out into the brew community in a much more visible way in the future.

Thirsty Planet Brewing Company

Thirsty Planet Brewing Company opened its doors in 2010. It's owned by Brian Smittle, who found his way somewhat haphazardly into craft beer. While studying British politics in England, he took a night off and made his way to a pub nearby. As many brave beer adventurers before him have done, he pointed to a tap on the wall gleaming through the smoke of the pub and said "gimme that one" without a whole lot of thought or the context to qualify the beer he had ordered. The bartender pulled his beer from a beer engine (a machine used to pump beer from a cask), which stood out to Smittle, as he waited. He stepped away from the bar, sat down with his beverage, took a sip and fell in love. He loved it so much that he moved back to the States, changed his major to business administration and started homebrewing.

After graduating, but before he was ready to take on things like "a real job"—a man after our hearts—Smittle spent some time in Vail, Colorado, at a local beer festival. One local brewery in particular, called the Hubcap, caught his attention, so the next day he made his way to the brewery to volunteer his time and ask questions. As he walked into the space, he was surprised and excited to see a room split by a wall of glass. On one side of the wall, the brewer was mixing the mash for a 260-gallon batch of an English brown. On the other side, people were enjoying beers brewed in a similar way just a few weeks prior. This immediately struck Smittle and stuck with him as he cultivated his aesthetic for connecting with his own customers. He approached the brewer and began a conversation, during which he asked, "So, do you get paid to do this?" The brewer answered in the affirmative.

And then Smittle's head exploded.

The head explosion might be a little historically inaccurate, but that brewer's statement resonated with not only Smittle's passion for craft beer, which he had been developing since his time in England, but also the future he wanted to build for himself personally. It set him on a defined path and showed him the end goal he'd been lacking when he made his way to Vail. He began volunteering and later took a position at the brewery to hone his brewing skills and familiarize himself with the working pieces that make a brewery thrive.

In the early '90s, while giving a tour of the brewery to a group of college students from Oklahoma, the group approached him with an offer of an ownership piece of a brewery they were starting up. He accepted the offer and, in 1993, helped open the doors to the brewery. It was vastly successful. Within a few years, his brewery had opened not only the main brewing facility but also four satellite stores selling the beers it was producing around the area. However, Smittle missed the days spent in his rubber brewing boots. The growth of the business had taken him from the dream of skiing in the morning and then brewing 'til dawn, so he and his wife sold their share of the business and set off in search of a new place they could open the brewery that he'd imagined, settle down and start a family.

Volunteers pour beer in the Thirsty Planet taproom. *Holly Aker.*

Thirsty Planet's Ben Sabin and girlfriend Amy Johnson pour beer at the 2013 Texas Craft Beer Festival at the Dancing Bear Pub in Waco, Texas. *Holly Aker.*

Although it lacks the skiing, Austin was a particularly fitting candidate for such endeavors, so it was with very little hesitation that the couple made their way down south.

"I think people [in Austin] want to reconnect with the food and things they consume," Smittle said.

So Smittle built a space where people in Austin could enjoy his beer. Similar to Hubcap Brewery he'd visited and worked at years before in Vail, Smittle's brewing facility for Thirsty Planet is situated in the lovely rolling hills west of the city and features a beautiful tasting room that is warm and inviting. As the place of conception for *Bitch Beer*, we are very familiar with how approachable that space makes craft beer. The paramount feature that draws people in is a glass wall set just behind the taps allowing tasters to see into the brewery itself as the wares they enjoy are created before them. However, it's been a struggle for the brewery to keep up with the production. It is always adding more kegs, more fermenters and more hours to get its business done. This constant race to get ahead of the demand has also given the team the greatest satisfaction.

"With mostly four people working it has been a tremendous joy to see just how far we have come in only three years. Its amazing to really see this bird fly," Smittle said.

Thirsty Planet's beer portfolio is composed of a number of staple flagship beers like Yellow Armadillo wheat beer, Thirsty Goat amber and Bucket Head IPA.

"We see beer as one of the most social things on the planet. More people come together and share life experiences over a beer than arguably coffee or tea," Smittle said. "We are flattered when it's our beer that is bringing people together; we feel like we are part of that conversation and part of those life events."

The team at Thirsty Planet strives to make its beers sessionable and approachable, while staying true to the styles it brews. Having enjoyed more of each of Thirsty Planet's flagship representatives than we could count, we can vouch for how balanced and deceivingly drinkable these beers are, even those with a higher ABV hidden in the hops and malt.

The brewery also features a really dynamic list of seasonal beers. The flavors they develop in these brews are innovative and highly crafted spinoffs of classic beer pairings. Jittery Monk, for example, is a coffee-infused dubbel, but instead of simply taking the coffee (procured from local roaster Kohana Coffee, of course) and adding it to the beer in the finishing tanks, Smittle and his team smoked the local coffee beans at Franklin's Barbecue, another Austin staple, to bring some very subtle nuances of smokiness to the coffee. Then, they went back and asked the folks at Kohana to cold brew the smoked beans and send the coffee back to the brewery. Slowly, as in two gallons at a time slowly, the team integrates the coffee into the dubbel as it finishes in the bright tanks, checking the flavor after each addition and carefully monitoring the evolution of the beer until the profile is just what they are looking for. It is an outstanding product. The careful decision making and attention to detail come through in a very balanced and totally delicious seasonal beer. It has a great coffee taste but finishes with that malty sweetness beer lovers search for in a dubbel. Other seasonals, such as the pumpkin ale Magic Harvest, Franklin's smoked porter and Silverback ale, also embody that meticulous craft and local-centric focus.

By the end of 2013, Thirsty Planet plans to release its beers in bottles.

"Expect us to continue to be embedded in our community and supporting it in many different ways. And expect new and unique styles from around the planet. We are proud of everything we have done and we could not have done this without the great support of our community here in Austin. Everything from our volunteer help to support from family and friends," Smittle said. "We are happy to support a different charity every other month (even though the money isn't a lot). And we are happy to help nourish brewing growth and education whether it is a homebrewer or someone starting a new brewery in the area."

Mostly, we look to the team to keep our planet thirsty.

CHAPTER SIX
NEW KIDS ON THE BOCK

PAIRS WITH ROGNESS ROOK SCOTCH ALE

The craft beer community in Austin hit a growth spurt starting in 2011—a huge growth spurt. If the community were a woman, it would have started as your little neighbor girl. In 2010, it was just a skinny preteen with pigtails, but after 2011, it was that girl who came back after summer break a foot taller, no braces and kind of hot. Between 2011 and 2013—at least until the day of our publishing deadline—eleven breweries opened in Austin. Fun fact, there were only ten breweries when we first started writing this book, but one last brewery had its grand opening in the few months of this book's development, further proving the incredible growth the city is seeing.

With craft beer's popularity skyrocketing, these breweries established in the years since 2010 found themselves in the position where they were able to stretch their legs and go a little crazy. Tex-Mex style beer? Definitely. A spinach-alfalfa beer? Sounds awesome. An horchata milk stout? Who wouldn't drink that? And Austin craft beer drinkers are lucky enough to sit back and enjoy the ride as Austin's mad beer scientists go to work.

JESTER KING CRAFT BREWERY

Located in the Hill Country just outside the Austin city limits, Jester King Craft Brewery sits on arguably the most beautiful setting for a brewery in the city. We're not ones to have a wedding Pinterest board, but even we'd put Jester King on one. The brewery and taproom are housed in an old renovated hangar, and just a couple hundred feet away is a covered pavilion complete with a stage, antique chandeliers and picnic tables—perfect for day drinking at Saturday tasting hours, parties and, perhaps, even weddings. Surrounded by tall trees, open fields and plenty of shaded seating, both buildings sit on a few acres of land that the brewery rents from a rancher—a location that head brewer and coowner Jeff Stuffings just stumbled on.

"We were planning on being somewhere closer to downtown, probably being in some industrial park, but we got a call out of the blue from the rancher here," Stuffings said. "This ranch is about 220 acres; our property is a relatively small portion of it—a 4-acre plot. When we came out and the rancher mentioned the possibility of us building out here, we were pretty excited about it."

Stuffings and the other owners—Ron Extract and Stuffings's brother, Michael Steffing—had no idea at the time, but choosing this remote location turned out to heavily influence the style of beers they brewed. Stuffings got his start in craft beer by homebrewing while he was in law school, and like many brewers, what started as a hobby eventually blossomed into a passion he wanted to pursue professionally. Stuffings and his brother began the planning process for Jester King in 2008 and were joined by Extract a year and a half later. Stuffings and his brother were originally planning on sticking to an Anglo-American style of brewing, but Extract, who had a background in importing and distributing, persuaded the brothers to explore new styles of beers.

"The combination of finding this location here in the Hill Country and then also having Ron introduce us to some of these really wonderful beers from around the world influenced us to focus more on the farmhouse and wild style of brewing, the more Franco-Belgian in origin," Stuffings said.

The Hill Country's influence came in the form of yeast. While Jester King's primary fermented beers, including Noble King and Le Petit Prince, use a farmhouse yeast strain from Brasserie Thiriez in northern France, its barrel-program beers use yeast straight from the land.

"We've done a number of experiments over the years where we've harvested yeast from flowers, from berries, from open air fermentation and cooling beer overnight in a coolship and taking those strains and using them to create interesting flavors as the beer matures in oak," Stuffings said. "As well as [using] native bacteria, which provides the souring qualities to the beer."

When Jester King first opened, a few but not all of Stuffings's beers were brewed in the farmhouse style. However, not too long after the opening,

Head brewer and coowner Jeff Stuffings gives a Saturday afternoon tour of the Jester King barrel room. *Holly Aker.*

Stuffings and the rest of the Jester King crew decided to switch all their recipes to include farmhouse yeast and to brew in this style.

"We were told by a lot of brewers starting out that without more Anglo-American style beers in your portfolio, it's going to be hard to do business in a state like Texas," Stuffings said. "We like those beers and have an appreciation for them, but ultimately, once we got going and gained more confidence to brew to a little more niche style of brewing—the Franco-Belgian Farmhouse ales and wild beers and sour beers—we just decided... to focus on this style of brewing."

What drew Stuffings to the farmhouse style of brewing was the dimension and sophistication with which these beers are imbued. Since Stuffings got his start in brewing as a homebrewer, his original introduction to flavor in beer came from malt, hops and adjunct ingredients. However, farmhouse beers taught him that flavor can come from so many other places.

"To me the idea of what a complex beer [was] used to be [if] it had coffee and chipotle peppers in it and this and that spice; therefore, it must be complex," Stuffings said. "I've really changed my opinion drastically where now, to me, complexity is not so much along the lines of malt and hops, although I love flavors from those ingredients, but more through just fermentation. The most interesting and enjoyable flavors that I've experienced in the beer world are a product of simple fermentation. Different organisms performing different chemical processes on sugars and dextrins and starches and proteins."

Another good way to add complexity to beer that Jester King discovered is to collaborate with breweries that share or have a similar beer vision as you do. On any given Saturday, you're likely to find several guest beers on tap in the Jester King taproom, and oftentimes, one of these beers is from Mikkeller, a Danish craft beer brewery that is making some of the most well-respected and delicious beers in the world. Besides pouring various Mikkeller beer, Jester King and Mikkeller have collaborated on several beers—Drink'in the Sunbelt and Beer Geek Rodeo, which is the Texas version of Mikkeller's Beer Geek Brunch. Beer Geek Rodeo was also the base for Jester King's Weasel Rodeo and Whiskey Barrel Rodeo.

So how did a small brewery located in the boonies of Austin get the chance to team up with the renowned Mikkeller? It was a feat accomplished with a little luck and a lot of bro time. In 2009, when the Jester King crew caravaned up to Chicago for the Craft Brewers' Conference, the brewers crashed in the flat above their friend's liquor store, West Lakeview Liquors. When they got to the flat, they found out they were going to have some roomies: Mikkel Bjergsø and Thomas Schøn of Mikkeller.

"We got to hang out with those guys for a week and got to know them and talked about brewing together," Stuffings said—aka, bro time. He continued:

> We didn't even have a functioning brewery then; we were just a brewery in planning. It's kind of funny in a way because they're a European, Danish brewery that is very American inspired. Their beers definitely have a lot of American inspiration, and they often talk about 3 Floyds being one of their biggest sources of inspiration. We, on the other hand, are an American brewery that really draws a lot of inspiration from classic European-style brewing, so it's kind of weird to have an American and European collaborating together although drawing influences from the opposite of each other.

Obviously creativity and originality are two of the biggest components of every Jester King beer. And its latest experiment is no different. In February 2013, Jester King brewed two spontaneous batches of beer in a coolship. A cool what in the where now? A coolship is basically just a big wooden box with no cover that collects bacteria from the environment. No yeast is added, so fermentation occurs naturally from whatever airborne yeast falls in.

"We're not calling it lambic out of respect to traditional lambic brewers," Stuffings said. "Although we really did try to stay true to the classic lambic way of making beer where our grist was just raw wheat and pilsner. We used aged hops, did a tub of mash and right after boiling racked the wort to a coolship."

Spontaneous brewing can only be done in colder months when temperatures lend themselves to having the type of required organisms in the air and the actual cooling of the wort overnight. And this is Texas, so that gives you about two days out of the year. Luckily, Jester King took advantage of those days and got its spontaneous fermentation in. But don't plan on getting your hands on this spontaneous libation anytime soon. The beer has to sit for two years before the brewing process is complete. Ugh, patience is so overrated.

However, if all goes well, these spontaneous beers could become a regular thing around the Jester King compound.

"It's still a ways off, but we're getting ready for…December," Stuffings said. "We're going to hopefully not just do two batches but twenty, twenty batches this winter. We don't want it to be this side project. We'd love it to be a major part of what we do."

Spontaneous fermentation in a coolship is a pretty seldom-used brewing tactic here in the good ol' U.S.A. In fact, Stuffings was able to name all the breweries that are also spontaneously fermenting their beers on one hand.

"There's only a small handful that I'm aware of," Stuffings said. "There's Allagash in Portland, Maine, and Anchorage Brewing in Anchorage, Alaska. I don't know of anyone else besides those two that have a coolship."

Besides tinkering with his new and exclusive coolship, Stuffings is currently working on several new sour fruit beers. The first, which was officially announced in May 2013, is a barrel-aged sour beer with raspberries named Atrial Rubicite.

"The name means a raspberry parasite of the heart," Stuffings said. "It basically means the raspberry has taken over the heart of the beer. We took some farmhouse ale, we soured it for about a year in oak and then, for the last three months of fermentation, we added raspberries."

Stuffings was generous enough to crack open a bottle of Atrial Rubicite during our interview, and we can attest to its amazingness. Like most Jester King releases, the beer has a very dry taste with a nice balance between sweet and sour. Definitely a beer you'll want to go back to for seconds, maybe even thirds. Atrial Rubicite and the rest of the sour fruit beers to come will be packaged in smaller bottles—five hundred milliliters—than most Jester King beers, and each will be brewed with several hundred pounds of its fruit per barrel. Rumor has it a barrel-aged strawberry sour beer is up next. It will most likely already be on shelves by the time this book comes out, but if not—surprise!

As for the future of Jester King, the brewery plans on changing its license to a brewpub now that the laws have changed so that brewpubs can distribute their beer. But in the meantime, it is making a few changes to the way its Saturday tastings and tours are run. According to the brewery's blog, starting June 29, it will be selling its beer by the glass.

> [The new laws allow] visitors to our brewery to experience a greater diversity of what we make at Jester King…Previously, there had been an odd disincentive for us to offer our most limited beers to brewery guests because doing so would have cut down on the quantities that we had available to sell. That is no longer the case, and visitors to our brewery will now be able to drink our more limited beers.

The only downfall to this change is that Jester King is no longer able to serve beer from other breweries. So say goodbye to Mikeller and all the other guest beers that were so common to the brewery's taproom. But don't pout too long because before you know it, Jester King will shift over to brewpub status, and it has a lot of exciting events planned for when that happens.

Hops & Grain

When Josh Hare decided to open a brewery, the beer was, of course, the first thing on his mind, but coming in at a very close second was a value most brewery owners don't think about right at the beginning: sustainability. To Hare, sustainability comprises the environment, the community and the culture.

"I spent a bulk of my time in college backpacking on my own," Hare said. "I'd take my dog out, and we'd go for two weeks in the Front Range of Colorado. In that, I spent a lot of time on trails that had been developed. And they were littered, and they were dirty. There were people out there smoking cigarettes on the trail. It was very frustrating to me."

That feeling stuck with Hare, and when it came time for him to define the character of his brewery, the environment was the first thing on his list. He

No surprises here: award-winning beer personality Jake Maddux (far left, in hat) spends yet another Friday at the Hops & Grain taproom. *Caroline Wallace.*

wanted to make a beer that wasn't just beneficial to sober patrons but was also beneficial to the environment.

Hare is a people person, and he wanted to make sure his beer and his brewery made a positive impact on the community. His final value was culture, meaning putting an emphasis on the individual in order to produce a product that is one of a kind. He'd seen companies that operate as if on a formula—action A plus action B equals profit—but he wanted to build a company that operated from the heart.

With these three values as the driving force behind his brewery, Hare needed a succinct word that communicated how they fit together. Eventually he landed on sustainability.

"What we're trying to do with the environment is add sustainability," Hare said. "What we're trying to do with our community is create a more sustainable model. Then in our industry, we're trying to do something that we believe is a sustainable way to operate. So we came up with this tag line of 'Craft Beer Sustainability.'"

Hare has applied this concept to every aspect of the brewery, from buying new equipment and bringing in new ingredient suppliers to hiring new employees and structuring the company bonus system. For example, he chooses to package his beer in aluminum cans, as aluminum is the most wholly recyclable material, and he reimburses his employees for every day they use an alternative mode of transportation, which Hare defines as getting sixty-five miles per gallon or better.

Further vindicating its dedication to sustainability, Hops & Grain is a member of 1 Percent for the Planet. Through the organization, the brewery donates 1 percent of its annual revenue, which goes to the organization's network of more than three thousand approved environmental nonprofits worldwide. Even Hops & Grain's spent grain is used in a sustainable way. After the brewing process, Hare takes the used grain and makes dog treats called Brew Biscuits. While most brewers give their spent grains to cattle ranchers, using the grains to make dog treats contributes to sustainability by cutting out the wastes, such as fuel, incurred in transporting the grain.

"We personally as citizens, we're the ones responsible for the negative effects that happen," Hare said. "The more that we can do to reduce that, one, it's just the right thing to do, and two, it's a good model to display to other people."

Another unique aspect of Hops & Grain is its Green House program. While the brewery has three yearly beers—Alt-eration, a malty altbier that won the 2012 World Beer Cup Gold Medal for its style category; Pale Dog, a dry, hoppy pale ale that Hare brewed in honor of his beautiful golden retriever, Suzie; and the One They Call Zoe, a dry-hopped pale lager, which is the newest yearly beer and inspired by another one of Hare's dogs—the Green House program is Hare's creative outlet. Housed on a three-barrel system, the Green House lets him brew anything and everything he wants. Past creations have included an horchata milk stout, a Chardonnay cherry Alt-eration and a bourbon barrel–aged Alt-eration, which Hare lovingly dubbed "Mean Irene" on the request of his grandmother Irene.

By keeping the Green House supply small and limiting the distribution to only a very select number of bars around town, Hare feels he's adding to his mission of culture and community. Since the Green House beers change weekly, it encourages people to come out to the brewery, where they can try the beer, talk to the people who made it and get to know other craft beer enthusiasts.

"[The Green House] is not a money maker for us at all," Hare said. "We lose money on every batch of it we make in the Green House, but I designed it that way because it feeds our creativity and it gets people into the taproom. They know the first place it's going to be on tap is there. There's no other bar you can go to that has ten of our beers and drink them really cheap."

And Hare is right. Every Thursday through Sunday the brewery is packed with everyone from beer industry members to regular craft beer enthusiasts to craft beer virgins ready to say goodbye to their AB InBev ways. With a regularly changing wall of taps of some of the most innovative beers in Austin and a team of friendly and knowledgeable brewery employers, Hops & Grain is more than succeeding in its mission.

In April, Hops & Grain applied to change its license from a brewery to a brewpub in anticipation that the beer laws overhaul would pass the Texas Senate. Since those laws did go through, the brewery is waiting for the Texas Alcoholic Beverage Commission (TABC) to approve its request. When Hops & Grain gets the go-ahead to begin operating as a brewpub, it will begin selling six packs and kegs to go. Until then, the brewery is taking advantage of the new laws and has expanded its taproom hours and days and is now selling beer by the glass rather than by a buy-the-glass-and-the-beer-is-free system.

AUSTIN BEERWORKS

Austin Beerworks is living proof that dudes who drink together, stay together. Started in 2011, the brewery was founded by Will Golden, Michael Graham, Adam DeBower and Mike McGovern. However, not too long before that, all the guys were scattered across the country doing their own things in New York, Maryland and Texas. What brought them all together was the one thing they had in common: their friendship with DeBower. And we all know how unbreakable a true bromance is.

The longest friendship of the four is between Graham and DeBower. The two met and became friends when they were just snot-nosed middle schoolers in Austin. After graduating high school, they went their separate ways to college—Graham to Boulder and DeBower to Waco—but they stayed in contact and saw each other during holidays. But what really cemented their friendship was when they both started developing an interest in good beer, rather than that piss-water excuse for beer that college kids drink, like Keystone and Icehouse.

Austin Beerworks debuted Heisenberg German Kristalweizen for their second-anniversary party. *Holly Aker.*

"It was independently, but we both got into beer at the same time," Graham said. "He was in Waco, and I was in Boulder. So we'd visit during the holidays. Even just talking, 'Oh, have you tried this one? Tried this one? I'll bring some of this back.' So we developed an even deeper friendship over beer."

"A lot of Instant Messenger conversations," DeBower said. (#BeforeFacebook.)

One summer, DeBower took a little pilgrimage up to Boulder to visit Graham, and what was supposed to be a weekend trip turned into a six-day, all-out beer scavenger hunt throughout the city.

"It turned into a beer trip of visiting, I don't know how many, twelve, fifteen breweries," Graham said. "Going on all the tours and talking to all the employees. Everybody was so happy, and it just seemed like the coolest thing. That's what planted the seed of 'wouldn't it be cool to work in the industry.'"

After college, DeBower moved to New York, where he met another native Texan, McGovern. At a mutual friend's house party one night, the two guys ended up hanging out and bonding over typical dude stuff: drinking beer and eating weird shit.

"We were sitting around drinking some beers, drinking good beers, and trying to decide if we're going to eat a durian fruit, which is probably one of the most foul-smelling fruits in the world," McGovern said. "As we're discussing if we're going to eat this fruit and several beers later, Adam decided to eat the fruit. I did not. And we became good friends."

After that party, McGovern and DeBower began hanging out regularly, almost always with beer involved, and usually at their favorite local craft beer bar, George Keeley.

"The funny thing is, [George Keeley] was closer to my house than it was to his house, but he was there more than I was," McGovern said. "He'd have an hour-plus train ride to get there, and I'd have a fifteen minute walk."

"Forty-five minutes," DeBower said.

"Eh, depends on time of day," McGovern said.

"Split the difference," DeBower said.

"But it was a great beer bar," McGovern said. "We'd just meet up there, share some beers, and see what's new. They always had different taps. There was always some new beer to try."

McGovern and DeBower became regulars at George Keeley, joining the bar's Beer Club and making strong friendships that they still have today with other craft beer enthusiasts. In fact, DeBower spent so much time at the bar, he became the thirteenth member of the Beer Club. You can go to the bar to this day and see his name engraved on the wall. Or you can do it the lazy way and just google George Keeley.

DeBower met Golden when he got a job at Flying Dog Brewery. After making the firm decision that he wanted to work in the craft beer industry, DeBower put together his résumé and set out to find a brewery that would hire him. The only problem was that he had no real experience in craft beer. That is, unless you count drinking it, but we'd all be PhDs if that were the case. (#AmIRight?)

"I found a brewery in Frederick, Maryland, that wanted a guy with no experience, who would take a low-paying job with long hours," DeBower said. "I was fortunate enough to be smiled on by the head brewer then, a guy named Tim Deutsch. He offered me a job scrubbing floors, cleaning tanks and doing what it is that we do. That's where I got to meet Will Golden. He was the lead brewer at the time, and I was the youngest, newest cellar operator."

Golden eventually moved on to work at Barley and Hops Grill & Microbrewery in Frederick, Maryland, but the two remained friends and saw each other all the time.

"He used to come into my pub and harass me all the time," Golden said. "We'd drink way too many beers and go back into the brew house and screw around with shit. We just became really good friends and drank our asses off.

From there, we both discussed our pipe dreams of having our own breweries at some point."

Golden had always planned on starting a brewery with his brothers, but when that unfortunately fell through, he was delightfully surprised to get a call out of the blue from DeBower. DeBower had moved back to Austin and was working at Real Ale Brewing in Blanco. While he was brewing beer in the Hill Country, he was also brewing something else at the same time—a plan to open his own brewery. DeBower told Golden about Graham and McGovern and asked him to come on down to Texas so the four of them could meet and talk about this crazy idea of opening a brewery.

Golden agreed and made the journey to the Lone Star State just in time for them to have their first meeting at the Real Ale anniversary party that year. Which anniversary it was exactly is still up for debate, probably a side effect of all the beer that was consumed at the party. Oh, and the heatstroke Golden had that day as well. Besides that little drawback, the meeting was a success. All four guys hit it off and immediately began the huge planning process of starting a brewery.

In 2011, Austin Beerworks opened up shop in North Austin. The guys started with four beers: an extra pale ale, a pilsner, a schwarzbier and an IPA. Peacemaker, the extra pale ale, is the lightest and easiest to drink of the four, according to Golden. While most people expect a kick of hops, the beer has a strong malt flavor and is brewed with oats and three different kinds of hops. Pearl Snap is the brewery's German-style pilsner, as well as its top-selling beer. Unlike most pilsners, Pearl Snap is dry hopped to give it an American twist, but it's still very drinkable with low bitterness, making it a perfect companion for tubing down the river. The schwarzbier—or black lager—is appropriately titled Black Thunder. Golden was jazzed on the idea of making a schwarzbier because at the time, there were very few, if any, breweries in the country producing one. Black Thunder is made by simply taking Pearl Snap that hasn't been dry hopped and adding debittered black malt. Their final yearlong beer is Fire Eagle. When coming up with the recipe for Fire Eagle, Golden wanted to make an IPA that was made for Texas, so he kept the bitterness, as well as the ABV (at 6.5 percent), low. However, Fire Eagle is dry hopped so it has a very rich, hoppy fragrance.

Besides making awesomely brewed beer, Austin Beerworks is also known for its awesomely designed cans. In 2012, at the Craft Brewers' Conference, the guys took home two awards: Best in Color for Pearl Snap and second place for Best Overall Design for the whole lineup, with Fire Eagle as the representative. They've also won several European awards for their designs

Cans of Austin Beerworks Pearl Snap and Black Thunder feature award-winning designs from Helms Workshop. *Holly Aker.*

as well as two different recognitions in *Communication Arts*, a top-notch design magazine, which Graham said was like the equivalent of a Great American Beer Festival award for designers—meaning super prestigious.

Austin Beerworks can thank a local dude named Christian Helms, who owns a studio in town called Helms Workshop, for all these badass designs. Before working with Helms, none of the Austin Beerworks guys had ever met him, but it was bromance at first beer. McGovern even said he refers to him as the fifth partner.

"He's just an awesome human being who each of us loves to hang out with," DeBower said. "We didn't know him before we started the project. The first time we met him, it was going to be a fifteen-minute meeting. Turned into a three-and-a-half-hour drunken bro-down. The second time it was the same story: it was supposed to be fifteen minutes, but it was like three hours of beers. The third time, he was like, 'Seriously, we've got to stop doing this.'"

"It was like, 'My wife is going to leave me,'" Golden said, jokingly, of course.

Once the "meeting" ended and the guys actually got to talk about their design vision, they learned they were all on the same page. Besides the four mainstay beers, Helms has branded every bit of Austin Beerworks: the website, the seasonal beer cans, the shirts, stickers, koozies, growlers, underwear. (Just kidding. There's no Austin Beerworks underwear—yet.)

One reason for this lack of Austin Beerworks undergarments is the greater demand for something else: beer, duh. In 2012, Austin Beerworks was the third-fastest growing brewery in the country. According to the *New Yorker*, the brewery went from producing 1,051 barrels in 2011 to 5,188 in 2012. That's a 394 percent increase. So how are they keeping up with the demand?

"We aren't really," Golden said.

"The one thing we won't compromise on is quality," McGovern said. He elaborated:

> One of the key things of not compromising on quality is making sure you have good people who are trained. We'll grow as fast as we can as long as we bring in good people, people you want to spend the entire day with, get them trained, make sure they really know what they're doing, someone you're willing to trust your business with. That actually is what really controls our growth. The rest of it we can work around, but having solid, core people and not compromising quality is what determines the rate of growth.

As Graham explained, they aren't looking for just anyone when hiring someone new; they're looking for that perfect person. They've turned down experienced brewers in the past when they felt he wouldn't fit in with the culture they've created.

"Culture is very important to us," Golden said. "We didn't start this thing to make a million bucks or even become wealthy. We do it because we really love it. Culture to us, next to the beer quality, is the most important thing. Keeping our employees happy, doing fun things with them and just trying to make this an awesome place to work [is our goal]."

Besides ensuring the staff is up to par to deal with the increasing popularity, the guys are constantly expanding the actual brewery in order to meet its high demand. Its rate of expansion has been so steady that Austin Beerworks added new tanks four different times over a period of fourteen months.

And it's on track to keep this crazy growth spurt going. As of July 2013, they had produced more than four thousand barrels of their delicious libations, which will put them somewhere close to nine thousand barrels by the end of the year. What makes that even crazier to think about is that they don't distribute outside Austin. The bar farthest away that carries their

Above: Austin Beerworks's wall mural showcases the brewery's signature Fire Eagle "Screeeeeeee" motto. *Holly Aker.*

Left: Austin Beerworks's new IPA series Heavy Machinery takes its name from the common surgeon general's warning. We're guessing they would probably advise against cats drinking it as well. *Holly Aker.*

beer is the Barber Shop in Dripping Springs. That means Austinites will have consumed about nine thousand barrels of Austin Beerworks beer come 2014. Way to go, team.

Currently Austin Beerworks has an IPA series out called Heavy Machinery. The name and the whole idea behind the beer and the packaging came from yet another drunken bro-down sesh with Helms and another creative mind, Mike Woolf, who writes a lot of copy for the brewery and makes their videos, which apparently are unfit for consumers' eyes. You know what that means, wink, wink.

"We were having beers at Banger's [Sausage House & Beer Garden] and discussing where we want to go, what new, cool stuff we should do and had a bunch of beers," Golden said.

"We started talking about the surgeon general's warning," DeBower said. "How funny it would be if the whole label was just the surgeon general's warning, and we were like, 'How about our own warning? Why don't we call it Heavy Machinery.'"

All the guys love IPAs, and since they only have the one, they thought this would be a good chance for experimentation. So they started with a black IPA in the spring of 2013 and then moved on to a double IPA in June. July 2013 will see a half IPA, which Golden explained is basically an aggressively aromatic pale ale. In total, the series will have eight different IPAs, including an English-style, a Belgian-style and a wet hop IPA.

Looking into the future, the guys plan on adapting the brewery to fit the new beer laws that were passed this year, which now allow for them to sell their beer to thirsty patrons on site.

"We definitely want to have people in the brewery more often," Graham said.

"Probably some more investment in the taproom, making it more comfortable," DeBower said. "More investment in people, more employees potentially."

However, they don't expect to change their taproom and tasting hours' deal of buying the glass and getting tickets for several pours of beer. The only thing that may change is moving those hours to Saturday and instead hosting a happy hour at the brewery on Friday evenings.

"It's funny, but it almost feels nostalgic now," Graham said. "How we had to sell a tour and a glass with free beer. It would be sad to give up."

FLIX BREWHOUSE

Flix Brewhouse has probably the most interesting concept of all the breweries in town. Besides being a brewpub that serves food and beer, it's also a movie theater. Patrons can come to Flix, watch a movie and be served delicious food and tasty beer that's made right there by head brewer Justin Rizza.

Rizza didn't start off wanting to be a brewer; he wanted to be a chef. He started cooking at age sixteen and worked his way up, eventually becoming a sous chef. As he was about to leave for culinary school in 1999, he had a drastic change of mind. While he loved cooking and the excitement of the kitchen, he wasn't sure if the long nights and weekends were part of the life he wanted. So he quit his job, sold his car, bought a van and went traveling around by himself. After a few months, he came back to his hometown of Denver and began looking for a job, particularly a job at a brewery.

"I was just really starting to appreciate good beer," Rizza said. "I love making things. I really didn't know anything about the brewing process, but I just thought, 'How awesome would that be?' So I started calling around to every brewery in town. Breckenridge Brewery was actually the one that ended up hiring me to clean kegs and filter beer and fill orders."

From there Rizza worked his way through quite a few breweries. The Breckenridge location where he got hired closed down a few months after he started, and after making snowboards for a short period of time at Never Summer Industries in Denver, he landed a job at Great Divide Brewing Company.

"I was running the bottling line there," he said. "Doing a lot of solo work. Pretty much doing everything but brewing. Obviously Great Divide has had tremendous success, but I think there were seven of us at the brewery at that point. I think it was a fifteen-barrel system, and they were brewing three times a day."

After a while, Rizza and his wife, Carrie, decided they needed a change of scenery. They both had lived their entire lives in the Denver area, so they started thinking about somewhere they could go. And of course this new city had to have an awesome beer scene. Eventually, they settled on Seattle. Once they were settled into their new home in the city of rain, Justin got a job at Hales Ales.

"I backtracked a little bit," he said. "I started doing some part-time bottling and working my way back up. I ended up brewing there for about six years. It's a really cool brewery, doing open fermentation. Sixty-barrel open fermenter. It's Northwest English-style ales. That was a really great experience. I learned a lot there. I worked with some of the veterans of the Northwest brewing scene."

At the same time, he was also lending a hand to Baron Brewing, which made German-style beers. After spending several years in Seattle, Justin and Carrie had a kind of crazy idea.

"We realized we'd never be able to afford a house in Seattle ever," Justin said. "So we had this wild idea: let's just go move to Europe. Because people just do that, right? For me it fizzled off a couple days later; for my wife, not so much. She was like, 'No, we're going to pack, and we're going to do this.'"

So Justin began figuring out how he could make this work. After doing some research he learned that because his ancestors were from Italy, he could get dual citizenship. But it would take a lot of work and research. Justin and Carrie then moved to Tucson, Arizona, to live with Carrie's mom while they gathered all the paperwork needed, had documents translated and got everything official through the government. While they were there, Justin also took up his fifth brewery job working at Nimbus Brewing Company.

After they saved up enough money, they set off for Europe. They spent several months traveling all over the continent and eventually made their way down the boot of Italy. Justin had done some research ahead of time and set up some interviews at breweries in Tuscany and Sicily, and after staying in Sicily for a few weeks, he decided to take a job at Birra Amiata in Arcidosso and returned to Tuscany.

"They're still doing really well," Justin said. "I got to introduce lots of beers. I did an American IPA, a porter, a Belgian golden ale with some local saffron. I did a rye beer with anise. They're still making most of them to this day as far as I know. It was definitely a very fun experience."

Although he never got his citizenship, Justin and Carrie decided to come back to the States, start a family and try to make it back to Italy another day. They picked Austin to settle down in because they had never been here but had heard a lot of good things. After a few months in Austin, Justin got a job at Independence Brewing Company as the head brewer. After two years there, he heard about a job at Flix Brewhouse, and he jumped at the opportunity.

"The brewpub thing had a lot of appeal, lots of freedom, lots of control opportunities," Justin said. "I get to make whatever I want. I've got six full-time beers. A blood orange wit called Luna Rosa, which is our most popular beer. I've got a nice light golden ale, an American IPA called Lupulust, got the 10 Day Scottish Ale, which is nice and smooth and malty but real sessionable. A beer called Satellite, which is a hoppy Belgian red.

It's kind of a beer that doesn't necessarily fit real securely in a beer style, but it's delicious."

He rounds off his in-house taps with an ever-changing seasonal. He also has a line called Flix Brewhouse Funkhouse series, which is beer that uses wild yeast or sours aged in barrels.

Flix Brewhouse is also a big supporter of the homebrew scene in Austin. They partner with three different homebrew clubs—the Texas Carboys, the Austin Zealots and the Round Rock Homebrewers Guild—and have a quarterly competition.

"I give them a style," Justin said. "Or I changed it up this last time. I gave them five styles to choose from, and they brew that and enter it to us. And we judge it and pick the winner, and they get to come in to Flix Brewhouse to brew it with me. Then it goes on tap on our tap wall until it's gone."

Looking ahead, Flix isn't planning on making any big changes to the operations considering the new laws that went into effect this year.

"It would be nice to get a few kegs around town," Justin said. "Our sister company is Homefield Grill. It's like two doors down, but the laws have changed in such a way that it's not terribly convenient. We'd still have to go through a distributor to sell a keg to Homefield Grill because we have guest taps and wine [at Flix]."

Their focus right now is expansion. Next year, Des Moines, Iowa, will see a Flix Brewhouse pop up in town, and then a third Flix will open up somewhere else in the country not too long after that, with more to come.

"There could be ten in the next five years," Justin said.

Unfortunately, not all the Flix team members would see these great plans come to fruition. On June 4, 2013, very sad news broke that Walt Powell, vice-president of operations for Flix Brewhouse, had passed away at the young age of thirty-three. Powell was a very involved and passionate member of the Austin craft beer community.

"He left an amazing impact for being only thirty-three years old," Justin said. "He is so well known, even nationally and internationally."

The first time Flix went to the Great American Beer Festival, Justin was very excited to introduce Powell to all the people he knew in Denver, but it turned into Powell introducing Justin to many more people. Powell was so in sync with the nationwide beer culture that he could find a friend no matter where he went.

"He was so devoted to the Austin beer scene," Justin said. "He was always on top of what was going to be here out of the ordinary, what he could possibly get here, even if not through the legal channels, but whatever he could possibly bring to Austin and to our place that beer lovers would just go crazy for. He was always fighting for that."

Besides beer, Powell was always trying to come up with new and exciting events at Flix and Homefield Grill, which he also managed. Firkin Fest, a festival at Flix held in April 2013 where brewers from all over the city brought their craziest, most inventive firkins, was Powell's idea, as well as all the beer dinners at Homefield.

To honor Powell, Justin is making a beer he named Saison de Walt, which he plans on making part of his mainstays.

"It'll have a little funk, super dry, crisp Saison with pink peppercorns dry-hopped with styrian goldings because that's what Orval uses and that was his [Powell's] favorite beer in the world," Justin said. "If it turns out the way I'm thinking it will, it's going to be pretty awesome."

Even though Powell is no longer physically with the community, his influence will continue to inspire and affect everyone who drinks a beer brewed in the ATX.

"He is a beer legend," Justin said. "Those are the two words I keep thinking of. He's just been one of the biggest proponents, both on the creative side, trying to get people beers they can't get anywhere else, and also on the legislative side. He was at all those meetings and pushing for these bills to go through. He was just a passionate beer lover."

Justin encourages everyone to come drink the Saison de Walt and tell a story about Powell. He hopes this beer will allow Powell to continue to spread his influence throughout the community.

ROGNESS BREWING COMPANY

Forrest Rogness was in the craft beer industry way before he opened up Rogness Brewing Company. As chapter four detailed, he's owned Austin Homebrew Supply since the '90s, but his interest in craft beer came even before that.

Rogness got his start in homebrewing in college at the University of Iowa. Once he got the hang of it, he got his girlfriend, Diane, who is now his wife, involved in the hobby. It started out with her helping him hold things or handing him things, but eventually, Diane developed her own love of craft beer and began homebrewing herself.

After a while, the couple moved from Iowa City to Austin, bought Austin Homebrew Supply in 1999 and turned it into the huge and highly respected homebrew store that it is today. But after doing that for five years, Forrest began to think about a different side of the industry: brewing professionally.

"It seemed like a natural progression," Forrest said. "I'd written about a thousand recipes for Austin Homebrew, and I knew what people were wanting and what styles were not really represented. The recipes [at Rogness Brewing Company] are not ones that are currently at Austin Homebrew."

Now with this idea of opening a production brewery in his head, he had to think of a way to convince Diane it was a good idea, so he did it in the most casual way. Lucky for Forrest, his wife is a badass.

"Diane and I were driving around on a Sunday, and I just threw the idea out there," he said. "And she said, 'Yeah, I always thought we should do that.'"

See? Total badass and a definite match made in beer heaven.

Although that conversation took place in 2004, they had to push back the brewery plans for a few years after they had a small addition to the family. But in 2010, they slowly picked back up their planning process and really got the ball rolling in 2011. In between the eight months when they secured their location and could actually start brewing in their building, Forrest had plenty of time to perfect the four mainstays before they opened in March 2012: the Rook, a Scotch ale; the Ost, a porter; Yogi, a chai-spiced amber; and Beardy Guard, which is, simply enough, a bièr de garde.

Since its opening, the brewery has added a few more to its year-round lineup, including a pale ale called Rattler; an IPL (India pale lager) named Boomslang, after another snake reference; and Bella, which is an easy-drinking Belgian-style golden. They also have a few beers in the works, including a summer seasonal dubbed Joie de L'été, or the joy of summer in French, which is a saison that features lemon zest and lavender flowers.

"We're trying to do styles that are underrepresented or not represented at all," Forrest said. "The ones that were represented, take them off on a new path and push the envelope a little bit and try to come up with some unique things."

Forrest strongly believes that there is a beer for everyone, and that's his goal with Rogness Brewing. He wants to make enough varied beers so that everyone can find his or her beer in his lineup, and he feels the best way to do this is to not limit himself.

"A lot of the new breweries say, 'I'm a Belgian brewery,' or 'I'm a Farmhouse brewery,' and that's all they do," he said. "But I think there's a beer for everyone, and I haven't even scratched the surface of what I want to make. I've been coming out with a beer every month, which is crazy in

Rogness Brewing's new thirty-brewers'-barrel brewhouse became operational in 2013. *Caroline Wallace.*

The Rogness Brewing team takes a break from serving beer at the 2012 Texas Craft Brewers Festival. *Holly Aker.*

the industry, but I'm having a lot of fun coming up with something new all the time."

Forrest's creativity, innovation and maybe even slight stubbornness to do his own thing are obvious in the beers he brews. He explained that people kept asking him to make an IPA, but commonality isn't his style. Instead, he made Boomslang, an IPL. And the people rejoiced.

Besides contributing creative beers to the Austin craft beer scene, Rogness Brewing has become a hub for the community. The brewery has begun hosting a monthly game night where people can come play some games, meet new friends and, of course, drink some Rogness beer. They're also starting to host concert nights with bands, private parties and crafting nights with knitting and crocheting.

Always the entrepreneur, Forrest hopes to expand his reach in the community even farther with his next related refreshment venture. A little while ago, he purchased the warehouse next to his, and recently, he received the permits from the government to start a cidery in the new building, which he hopes to have open by the fall.

"Coming down the road, we're going to be doing sodas," Forrest said. "We're going to be doing some hard cider, some mead and some wine drinks too."

He knows that there are some members of the craft beer community who might have some backlash as he wanders into other drinking realms. But he's prepared for that.

"I'm just trying to have fun," Forrest said. "If somebody else's idea of fun is a certain style of beer, then that's all the better, but I'm trying to make all sorts of styles and all kinds of beverages. Yogi is very popular, but we get really rave reviews, and then we get some people who just don't like chai. I'm never going to be able to make a beer that everybody likes, but I make lots of different beers to try to make a beer for everybody."

TWISTED X BREWING COMPANY

In Texas, and Austin especially, we love our Tex-Mex food. You can't go a few blocks in this city without running into some kind of Tex-Mex establishment. The only problem is there aren't many good beer styles that are brewed to pair well with Mexican food, unless you feel like slummin' it with a Dos Equis or Modelo. Jim Sampson and Shane Bordeau saw this hole in the market and decided they had the solution, so in May 2011, they founded Twisted X Brewing Company, the first Tex-Mex brewery.

Sampson, the head brewer at Twisted X, got his first start in brewing in 1995 with a Mr. Beer homebrewing kit. Unfortunately, that first go-round turned out bad, really bad—so bad that he threw the kit out and figured he'd never brew beer again. Luckily, a little later, he made some friends who homebrewed in the more traditional stovetop method, and after hanging out with them more and more, he started homebrewing again and had a much better experience.

Bordeau had a similar first experience with beer. While he was in college in the early '90s, he tried his luck at homebrewing with his roommates and brewed an unfiltered beer that disgustingly tasted like chocolate milk. After that disaster, he admitted defeat and gave up on the venture.

Then in 2000, the two met while working at the same tech company and began hanging out and doing adventure races together that included mountain biking, kayaking, canoeing and other activities of the sort. Then, when Bordeau found out Sampson was brewing beer as well, he wanted in.

"I started hanging out at his garage quite a bit," Bordeau said. "Jim was a pretty good tequila connoisseur, and we had a bottle of Chinaco tequila one night. And slowly, as the night progressed, we got more and more bold. At that point, we had already discussed, 'Let's go build a brewing company. Let's go do something, but we have to make it different.' A little bit under the influence of tequila, we started talking about making a Mexican-style brewpub."

Their original plan was to find a Mexican restaurant that was already established and just add a brewhouse to the side of it. Sampson and Bordeau were so thrilled with this drunken idea that they immediately began planning their beer portfolio. Their first thought was lagers. They noticed that not many brewers make lagers, so they did a little investigating and found out the absence of lagers in the industry is because they take a lot of effort and a lot of time.

"It takes twice as long to make a lager because of fermentation," Bordeau said. "So we thought, 'All right, no problem.' We'll be a really small brewery. We'll make a lager that takes a long time, and we'll just come up with creative recipes that fall into that category."

After looking into the Texas Alcoholic Beverage Commision (TABC) laws, they nixed the idea of a brewpub. At the time, brewpubs could sell only their beer at the location it was made, and that didn't align with their master plan.

"[It used to be] if you make a brewpub like Uncle Billy's or North By Northwest, you sell your beer there and that's it," Sampson said. "So if I wanted to expand and sell my beer anywhere else, I have to build another one. I don't want ten restaurants throughout the state of Texas; I want to make beer and be able to sell it."

They decided to turn their dream brewpub into a production brewery. They would still make their Mexican lagers, but they would instead market them to Mexican restaurants around town. The next step was designing their recipes. They knew these beers had to have craft beer values and use local ingredients but also stay true to the basis of a classic Mexican lager.

"We paid really close attention to the ingredients and the quality," Bordeau said. "We wanted to do an all-grain brewery. Most Mexican-style lagers use a heavy amount of corn, but we use just a small amount of corn. We source it from Richardson Farms, which is an organic farm just north of Austin. It was really just for flavor. What we pay for corn from that farm is double the cost of barley."

Currently the brewery makes six beers, counting their seasonals. Their mainstays include a premium lager, their flagship beer; Cow Creek, which is a dark, Vienna-style lager; and Fuego, a jalapeño pilsner.

"We tasted all the other chili beers out on the market, and most of them blow your mouth out," Bordeau said. "You want one beer, and then you're done. Jim and I thought, 'That's not a very good business model for a brewery, to make a beer that you only buy one of.' So we made it really light. It's a pilsner, but then you have a hint of jalapeño at the end of it."

Señor Viejo is their tequila-aged imperial black lager. It's a dark lager that's aged in tequila barrels, which were originally Jack Daniel's barrels. This process brings out the bourbon and oak flavors of the barrels as well as the sweetness from the agave in the tequila. Siesta, their summer seasonal, is made by taking Twisted X, the premium lager, and fermenting it with prickly pears that Bordeau and Sampson pick themselves. And finally they have Chupahopra, which is a hoppy IPA and their only ale.

Despite making six different beers, Twisted X started as one of the smallest breweries in the state at the time with a three-barrel system. In fact, Bordeau and Sampson refer to their operation as a nanobrewery rather than a microbrewery. The two only recently hired their first employee, but for the first two years, Sampson and Bordeau ran the entire brewery themselves on nights and weekends, while also juggling their day jobs.

However, they have some of the largest expansion plans in the city. In December 2011, the guys broke ground for a new brewery out near Dripping

Springs that will exponentially increase not only its physical space but also its beer production. Last year, it produced 47 barrels of beer; this year, it's aiming for 70 barrels, and next year in its new place, it is hoping for 1,500 barrels. After that, it plans on being up in the 5,000-barrel range. Besides just making more beer, the guys also recently purchased a bottling line, which they plan on making 50 to 60 percent of their output.

They've been making steady progress on the new building, and as of July 2013, they were at a little more than 50 percent construction. Right now, the goal is to finish construction in August, begin brewing in September and have a grand opening party in late October.

NAMASTE BREWING

In 1986, a little gas station and convenience store called Whip In popped up on the side of Interstate 35 in Austin. Owned by the Topiwala family, the store has gone through drastic changes over the years, including losing the fill-up station, adding a bar with a vast array of taps and a kitchen to serve delicious Indian food and becoming one of the best bottle shops in the city. In 2012, Whip In decided to make one more change: become a brewpub.

Namaste, the brewery part of the business, is run by head brewer Kevin Sykes and assistant brewer Ty Wolosin, and together, the two are making American-style beers with creative Indian-themed names. For Sykes, brewing was something he had always dreamed of doing professionally.

"When I was younger, I had a friend who helped me brew my first batch of homebrew, and I thought about it for the next ten or fifteen years," Sykes said. "One day, I decided to buy a homebrewing kit and started brewing. I was laid off about a week later and unemployed for about two years with nothing to do but make beer."

He started hanging out at Whip In a lot, and when he heard about Namaste opening, he applied, got the job and started brewing.

Wolosin, who also works for a local farm, started brewing beer when he was in graduate school at the University of Montana at Missoula. One of his fellow grad peers suggested the idea to him and gave him a copy of *The Complete Joy of Homebrewing* and a beer kit. While his first few batches were nothing to be proud of, he didn't let that stop him.

"I stuck with it and continued to do homebrewing," Wolosin said. "I even took some beers to the Farmers' Market, and if you made a donation to the farm, you could get a free beer. So I got people's feedback doing it that way, which is probably semi-legal. Who knows?"

After Wolosin got a job at Whip In as a bartender, he gave his beer to Dipak Topiwala, the general manager, to try. Topiwala enjoyed the beer and told Wolosin he could be one of the Namaste brewers if he got a brewery license.

For such a small brewpub, Namaste actually makes quite a few beers. Their most regular is the Brahmale, which is a post-colonial IPA.

"I use grapefruit peel and lemon grass as well as citrusy, yummy American hops," Sykes said. "It's a little bit over 9 percent. It's not too bitter; I like IPAs that are a lot smoother and have a lot more aroma as opposed to bitterness. That one we have on at all times."

The brewery's stout, the Shivastout, is another popular beer. Made with a little more alcohol than the brown ale, it has bourbon-soaked dates with Belgian yeast that gives it a nice dark character. The Parvati Pale, which is the first beer the brewers have made under 8 percent and one of their newest, is a simple pale ale with lime peel for more of a kick. Sita's Revenge, which is one of Syke's favorites, is a saison made with French farmhouse yeast. There's also the Vishnavitripale, a Belgian-style tripel with rosehips, and seasonals, such as the Austoner Weiss.

"It's a take on the Berliner Weiss," Wolosin said. "We don't do a sour mash. The tartness you're getting is just from the lactic acid addition and some acidulated malt in the mash. We'd like to get into doing a sour mash."

The guys also have a lot of creative freedom to brew whatever they want. One of these creative experiments was a spinach alfalfa beer for St. Patrick's Day.

"We wanted to make a green beer but use natural ingredients," Sykes said. "All the additions to our beers we source locally as much as we can. That's a big part of Whip In, and we're just trying to do the same thing on the brewing side."

The two guys brew all these beers on a small system, a very small system. A half-barrel system to be exact. But even with a small setup, they are constantly brewing, and they make it work. For the month of May 2013, they did ten barrels, and by the end of the year, they're shooting for eighty, which just shows their persistence and dedication to producing good beer.

"It's hard to keep up," Sykes said. "I'd like to keep five beers on all the time. I'd really like to have eight."

Since most of their time is spent trying to keep up with demand and keep beers on tap, Sykes and Wolosin might not know what the future holds, but they know it will include brewing more of their delicious brews. They do, however, want to get a bigger system, which Sykes said will happen; he just doesn't know when. Another idea they have is to be able to send kegs of their beers to special events around town or even to festivals in Dallas or Fort Worth.

SOUTH AUSTIN BREWING COMPANY

South Austin Brewing Company is a Belgian-style brewery located in, you guessed it, South Austin. Led by head brewer Jordan Weeks, the brewery aims to brew beers worthy of traditional European Belgian breweries. (#DreamBig)

Weeks got his first taste of craft beer when he was eighteen years old and living in Washington, D.C. The beer was a Chimay, and it was like nothing he had ever drunk before. After the first sip, he sought out all the craft beers he could find, which was a bit difficult at the time because bars in America carried three beers: Coors, Miller and Budweiser. He made it work, though, discovering imported beers, regional beers like National Bohemian and, eventually, Anchor Brewing Company.

Weeks moved to Austin in 1989 and got a job brewing beer at Hill Country Brewing and Bottling in 1997. A few years later, he got a job at Austin Homebrew Supply, where the owner at the time, Dave Bone, taught Weeks to homebrew. He eventually left the beer industry for a more corporate job, but after thirteen years of that, he had had enough. He decided it was time to make a profession out of his true passion, and he started raising money to open his own brewery.

Before he opened South Austin or even had a building, he knew he wanted to brew Belgian beers.

"Belgian's my favorite kind of beer," Weeks said. "I drink all of my friends' breweries' beers, and a lot of them are what I call the 'usual suspects,' which is an amber, a blonde, a wheat, a porter or a stout and a pale ale or IPA. I love those beers and I drink them all the time, but my favorite beers to drink are Belgian-style beers."

In February 2012, South Austin launched with two beers: a Belgian golden ale and a Belgian saison. A year and a half later, the brewery hasn't added any new beers to its lineup, but that was its plan all along.

"Our whole philosophy was to do one thing right," Weeks said. "Every brew system is unique, and a brewery, in order to make good beer, has to really know its brew system. Spending a year on a system with just two recipes allows you to have that kind of expertise and that kind of very deep technical knowledge about your unique system that you bought. That said, we're coming out with a Belgian lager in the next few months, and then in the winter, we'll have a strong Belgian ale."

Weeks also cited Fritz Maytag, the original owner of Anchor Brewing Company. According to Weeks, Maytag brewed two beers—the Steam and an amber—for years as he figured out his brewhouse.

"It's a tradition to do this kind of thing," Weeks said.

With the new beer laws now in place, Weeks has tons of plans for how to make his brewery a place people want to come and spend a lot of time. His first step is making more beers. Since he can sell beer by the glass now without having to create new labels for each beer, he plans on making many different styles of beer. Some of these beers include a Belgian stout with coffee, a bourbon barrel–aged saison and an oak-aged golden.

His second step is expanding the brewery to make it more of an event space. In November, South Austin bought the warehouse next to it, adding 6,700 square feet to the brewery. It'll soon be adding a stage that's wired for sound and video as well as another bar, all with the goal of creating an event space that rivals Stubb's and Antone's. The ETA on this massive project is the end of summer, a perfect time of year, as they'll be bypassing the atrocious summer heat.

"We'll be selling beer in [the brewery] in the meantime until the construction over there happens," Chris Oglesby, the director of events and tours, said. "All the bands will still be playing on the patio, and we'll still be serving out of the tap wall. We'll be selling by the pint as soon as possible."

South Austin is also looking into other ways to distribute its beer. It's currently looking into adding a canning line as well as smaller, 335-ounce bottles for its beer.

As for the Austin beer community, Weeks sees it more as a family than just a professional industry. In the eighteen years he's been in the community, he's developed really great friendships with other brewers and loves to give back when he can.

"We made this all happen together," Weeks said. "It's a fairly tightknit community. We donate many, many barrels of beer to all kinds of charities and events. And also we do charity events here. We're always open as an event space for the community."

PINTHOUSE PIZZA

Months before Pinthouse Pizza even opened its doors in Austin's Rosedale neighborhood, the city was swarming with buzz about a brewpub that would serve pizza and beer made by a former Odell Brewing Company brewer. Then in October 2012, the brewpub opened and not only met but also exceeded everyone's expectations. The pizza was delicious, a perfect balance of cheese and sauce with fresh toppings and creative specialty pizzas, such as the bahn mi pizza, which soon became a *Bitch Beer* favorite. And the beer was plentiful: forty-five taps of house-brewed, local, national and international beers, as well as several changing bottles of beer available.

The crazy man who left a prestigious brewery like Odell in Fort Collins to come to our little city is named Joe Mohrfeld, and he's not crazy but rather quite possibly an artistic genius. While Mohrfeld was at college in Mankato, Minnesota, a philosophy professor of his turned him onto homebrewing, and he really became passionate about the hobby when he discovered the histories behind beer styles, breweries and the different beer cultures across the country, as well as the artistic aspect of beer.

"Brewing to me became the first artistic medium that really made sense," Morhfeld said in an interview with *Bitch Beer* before Pinthouse opened. "I really wanted to write. I wanted to be a philosopher and write a lot. I like writing, but it never came as easy. But with brewing, the understanding of ingredients came really quickly. It just made sense."

Soon after that, Mohrfeld began exploring all the different craft beers he could find in his little town. One that particularly caught his fancy was Summit Brewing Company's Extra Pale Ale, a beer that he still considers one of his favorites today.

"The first time I had it, though, I wasn't really sure what I thought," Mohrfeld said. "It was so different from anything I had tried before it, but I found myself coming back to it over and over, realizing how much I liked the formal hop aroma and distinctive bitterness so many other beers lacked at that time. I was quickly hooked on hops and started seeking out any pale and IPA I could find."

As homebrewing and beer quickly took over his life, he took a job working at Northern Brewer Homebrew Supply. Here he could brew everyday, learn some great tips from his beer mentors, write his own recipes and read all about the science of brewing. A few years later, he graduated with a master's degree from Colorado State University in Fort Collins, and he knew the only thing he wanted to do was get involved in the craft beer industry. His

Pinthouse Pizza released Burro's Breakfast Mexican lager in the summer of 2013. *Holly Aker.*

Pinthouse Pizza has four mainstay beers, as well as rare and seasonal releases. *Shaun Martin.*

first plan was to just open his own brewpub in the city, but luckily, a friend convinced him to get a little more experience before diving in headfirst.

"I was fortunate enough to have the opportunity to shadow brewer Jeff Doyle at Odell and quickly realized I knew absolutely nothing about professional brewing," Mohrfeld said. "My one-week job shadowing opportunity turned into a six month 'internship'—I worked for beer—during which time I enrolled in a formal Brewing and Malting Science program and feverishly applied for brewing jobs around the country. Finally, a spot opened up at Odell, and I started working part time in packaging. Shortly after I started, the company started to go through some significant growth, and I began to work more on special projects, developing beers and helping with marketing and social media. I was quickly moving up the ranks and found myself as the head brewer overseeing an, at the time, fifty-thousand-barrels-a-year brewery."

While he loved his job, the people he was working with and the beer he was making, he started remembering that he had always wanted to be part of a neighborhood brewery or brewpub rather than a national operation. He began talking to some of his friends in Austin who had just that idea, and soon, he found himself living in Austin and designing his own lineup of beer.

Pinthouse Pizza has four mainstays: a session ale, a pale ale, an imperial dry Irish and an IPA. Calma Muerta, the session ale, is pretty hoppy compared to most beers in the style, using about two and a half pounds of lemony hops per barrel. Mohrfeld describes the pale ale, which he dubbed Irony Genny, as a classically inspired pale ale, meaning it's not hoppy like an IPA but rather something you could drink multiples of and still walk straight. Bearded Seal is a classic dry Irish stout with just a little more alcohol. Mohrfeld's mainstays wrap up with the Man O' War, an IPA. While it's not a punch-you-in-the-face IPA, Man O' War has some tropical fruit characteristics and low bitterness, making it very drinkable. Besides those four, Mohrfeld has a rotating IPA series called the Fallen Cask, and it was inspired by a story he heard about the origin of the IPA.

"Back when England was colonizing India, they would ship provisions down to their colonizers, and beer's obviously in there," Mohrfeld said. "At the time, they brewed pale ales, and they were really low in alcohol. But [the IPA] really developed because there was a ship leaving, and some casks fell off the ship. The dockworkers got them out of the sea in the harbor and tapped them, and they really liked that flavor. So I had this falling cask idea, and to me it meant that [an IPA] was never designed to be consumed. It was supposed to age on the sea; it was supposed to die down on bitterness, so you didn't really know what you were getting."

One thing that people either really love or not love so much about Pinthouse is that it has become known as a very family-friendly establishment. On almost any given day you can see families enjoying pizza together with mom and dad sipping on a brew and even sometimes birthday parties for little tots as all the parents sit back and relax with a beer. However, coming from a more developed craft beer community, Mohrfeld has some great insight on the topic:

Having only recently moved to Austin, I am still a bit confused by the distinction between "family-friendly" and "typical beer scene" and why the dichotomy exists to so many people. Coming from a scene in Colorado, where craft beer is so much a part of the culture, I never really felt like a brewery or brewpub wasn't a place you could bring your family. In Fort Collins, for example, on any given day in the tasting room at Odell, you would always find kids hanging with their parents. Craft beer is a lifestyle for people in places like Colorado, and going to a brewery [or] brewpub- or brewery-sponsored festival is very much a family activity. I think for craft beer culture to be an integral part of Austin living, then it has to continue the shift of becoming a lifestyle that all people can be a part of.

As for the future of Pinthouse, Mohrfeld and his partners don't intend to make any changes to their business plan any time soon. Because they now have the ability to distribute their beer, they will definitely look into the option, but since they just opened less than a year ago, they see no rush to change things quite yet.

"Eight months ago, we were brewing our first beers," Mohrfeld said. "Six months later, we nearly doubled capacity. We are still trying to keep up with demand in the pub, so for right now, we are going to keep focusing on making the best beers we can and having a good time drinking beers with everyone here at the pub."

INFAMOUS BREWING COMPANY

The newest kid on the block, Infamous Brewing Company, launched in March 2013. Even though it's been distributing for only a few months, it's already gotten its beers in an impressive sixty plus bars over the greater Austin area, San Antonio, Houston and Galveston.

For Josh Horowitz, cofounder and brewer at Infamous, the brewery wasn't his first venture into craft beer. Before Infamous, Horowitz owned and operated an online service called Beer Bouquet. He felt there were tons of gifts out there that were centered on flowers, fruit and candies, so he wanted to create one that was about beer and sports. The website let you pick your favorite sports team or seasonally themed bucket and pair it with beer and snacks. Then you could send this gift anywhere in the country.

Horowitz began selling more craft beer through Beer Bouquet, which inspired him to really explore the craft beer market and find his favorite styles. Upon finding beers like Sierra Nevada's Ruthless Rye and Real Ale's Devil's Backbone, he knew he was hooked. This exploration also led him to brewing small batches of beer in his kitchen sink, and eventually, he realized that's where his true passion lay.

"It was a logical progression for my passion in the world of craft beer," Horowitz said. "I was brewing at least once a week at [Beer Bouquet], and it seemed like everyone in the neighborhood would be there every day, drinking my beer instead of going to the local bar. I felt that I must have something really special for people to keep coming back."

Unfortunately for Beer Bouquet, Horowitz would eventually be faced with a tough decision: keep the website or start a brewery?

"[Beer Bouquet] was my first real struggle with TABC," Horowitz said. "I was the first to have a license to operate in this manner in the state, and it took forever to get someone to sign off. Unfortunately, it was not my last. [The TABC] wouldn't allow me to continue to run Beer Bouquet if I was going to open a brewery. So I had to pick which child I loved more [and] the brewery won."

As of July 2013, Infamous had two beers in the mainstays: an IPA and the Hijack. The IPA is a West Coast–inspired style with four hops, four malts and a ton of power. The Hijack is a cream ale, which holds a special meaning to Horowitz.

"It was a style I grew up on in the Northeast," Horowitz said. "When I moved here a few years back, I couldn't find one I wanted to drink, so we decided to create a craftier version of a cream ale. It was a style from the early 1800s. As people began to migrate south to warmer climates, they were not able to lager as effectively for lack of temperature and equipment. So they started to use half the components from an ale and half from a lager. With ale yeast at a slightly cooler temperature, they were able to brew an ale that mimicked a lager."

Left: Infamous Brewing debuted its brews at its grand opening party at Bangers Sausage House and Beer Garden. *Sarah Wood.*

Below: Infamous Brewing Company launched with an IPA and its Hijack cream ale. *Caroline Wallace.*

Infamous is planning on releasing a seasonal version of Hijack soon that includes flavors of peach and citrus. They also were pouring a delicious pumpkin ale at their launch party, so hopefully that will make a come back when the weather starts cooling down.

Even though the brewery has been open for only a very short period of time, Horowitz and the other members of the Infamous team are already looking forward to the future. Their first order of business is converting their license.

"We plan to convert to a brewpub license to take advantage of the new laws," Horowitz said. "We plan to open for tours and tastings in the next few weeks with hopes of filling growlers and selling bottles of specialty small-batch beer to go. At least until we hit that ten-thousand-barrel mark."

CHAPTER SEVEN
BUILDING BREWMUNITY

PAIRS WITH HOPS & GRAIN PALE DOG

The dramatic uptick in Austin breweries didn't happen right away. The thirst for craft beer in the heart of Texas developed slowly over a few decades—through a period of brewpubs to one of almost none at all—and after a handful of pioneering beer enthusiasts led the charge for locally made brews with Budweiser a forbidden term.

But once the match was struck, the fire burned fast and burns still. As William Bearden, manager at the Hops & Grain tasting room, explained it, the old saying that a rising tide raises all ships is only part of the reason for the craft beer boom. Yes, Austin breweries can stay afloat creating the sort of beer they want to drink because locals want to drink them, too, but it's more than that. One key reason breweries and brewpubs alike are thriving is simple: community.

Beyond the brewers themselves, there are also bloggers and writers, such as *You Stay Hoppy Austin* and *Austin Beer Guide* (and, of course, *Bitch Beer*), who spend much of their free time drinking and writing about beer. There are beer managers installed in many local bars, eager to help a craft beer newbie find just the right pint to kick back with on a Thursday night. And, of course, there are the drinkers who flood popular local places like Rainey Street's Craft Pride and downtown's Chicago House and keep the taps flowing.

Austin's always been a mecca of opportunity. It's the place to be to fulfill a dream of selling tacos out of a food truck window, running a theater that specializes in comedy improvisation or opening a coffee roasting company that imports only Brazilian beans. It's that way now with craft beer—so alluring a career path that even longtime Colorado brewers find themselves drawn away from the Rocky Mountains to the Hill Country, as Joe Mohrfeld was in 2012 to open a beer-and-pizza joint on Burnet Road with some friends. That's because brewing beer and drinking it isn't just a career path for many of Austin's brewers. It's a family. It's a way of life. And it's certainly not a competition, or at least not any serious one.

"The goal is to become one of the big beer cities of the United States, but how can we do that if we are all wanting to outdo each other?" Mohrfeld said.

It's a sentiment echoed over and over among the many tightknit members of the craft beer scene, from Bearden to longtime homebrewer Debbie Cerda.

Ever since 1993, when the Texas legislature OK'd brewpubs, craft brewing in Texas's capital city has created the sort of camaraderie Austin is well known for, only with shotgunned cans and words like "firkin" and "hops" swapped around as much as a pitcher of freshly tapped Einhorn.

Even though the law change inspired the likes of Copper Tank, Bitter End and other brewpubs, Cerda said Austin as a whole wasn't quite ready for the existence of craft beer, subsisting just fine on run-of-the-mill light American lagers from top macrobreweries.

"The laws might change, but that doesn't mean the culture does," she said.

It took trailblazers like Real Ale to enlighten the locals swigging macro-brew about the taste of a good pint, and later powerhouses like Independence to convince the newly converted that there could be more than one Austin beer. Once they were hooked, it was up to big-dreaming newcomers like Jester King, settled into the countryside just outside the city, to convey that going to a brewery was as natural an activity for social drinkers as going to a bar. When that happened, *Austin Beer Guide* cofounder Chris Troutman said, Austin began to become a bastion of craft beer in its own right, following the well-trod footsteps of places such as Portland, Fort Collins and Asheville.

Craft breweries turned Austin into the sort of city that Colorado brewers flocked to for a very specific reason. Obviously, some really good beer enticed them. But Live Oak HefeWeizen, Hops & Grain's Pale Dog and Thirsty Planet's Thirsty Goat wouldn't have ever enchanted our tongues without the people behind them: the brewers supporting, befriending and teaching one another and the beer enthusiasts who encourage them to keep it up.

Austin brewers gather for a photo at the Love Beer fundraiser in June 2013. *Caroline Wallace.*

Partygoers celebrate Austin Beerworks's second-anniversary event. *Holly Aker.*

"The Collective Voice"

A key reason Austin craft breweries are so united and the brewers are legitimate friends is the Texas Craft Brewers Guild, a statewide faction of forty-two breweries and twenty-one brewpubs that aims to promote the common interest of Texas craft brewers.

"The guild, only a few years old in its current form, had been a long time coming," Cerda said, "a necessity that provided brewers not only with an organized means to band together, but the funding to stay together and fight for their causes."

"I do think the formation of the guild has had a huge impact on the craft scene," she said. "I felt for a long time, seven or eight years, that we needed that because there's more power in the collective voice. There's a heck of a lot more power in money, too. Bringing the community together, you're able to affect the changes that are needed."

Among the changes Cerda refers to were the restrictive state laws that prevented breweries and brewpubs alike from growing in the way that breweries out of state have had little problem doing with proper funds.

Tourists from around the country would hear about Austin's burgeoning beer scene and would want to stop by the breweries expecting they could kick back with the brewers and a pint of beer, just as they could in other big beer cities. The brewers were friendly, but they legally couldn't sell their beer on site. Instead, visitors could buy a pint glass and receive sample pours that often weren't quite full.

Brewpubs had the opposite problem. They could sell their beer at the restaurant-brewery but couldn't package and distribute it for purchase elsewhere. The limitations for both breweries and brewpubs alike often meant they needed deep pockets to expand.

But one day in mid-June 2013, that changed when Texas governor Rick Perry signed into law a set of bills that comprehensively reformed the way beer is packaged and sold across the state. Because of so many votes from the Texas House of Representatives and the Texas Senate, the laws went into effect the second the ink from Perry's pen dried on June 14, and breweries across the state quickly adapted to the changes, celebratory pints in hand.

"The law change will help drive community in a way we couldn't see before," Mohrfeld, head brewer at Pinthouse, said.

His brewpub isn't interested in distributing its beers—fans will still have to head to the Burnet Road pizza place to get their fill—but he likes that

Pinthouse can now appear at festivals or sell kegs for special events, such as *Austin Beer Guide* release parties.

That's all due to the nonstop collaborative effort of groups such as the guild (the board of which Mohrfeld sits on) and Open the Taps, all lobbying hard to end the restrictions that, in a pro-business state like Texas, didn't make a whole lot of sense.

And the reform has been slow going. After all, it was only twenty years ago that brewpubs were finally permitted in Texas, just one reversal of dusty old laws dating back to Prohibition days (see chapter two).

Now, with the five new laws (SB 515-518 and 639), there is much more brewers and consumers can do—as well as cannot do. SB 639 was a controversial addition some organizations, including Open the Taps and Jester King Brewery, felt took away from the sweetness of the other victories.

Breweries can now sell beer on site—as much as five thousand barrels per year, which for many Austin breweries is more than half of their annual total production—although consumers can drink it only there, as taking beer to go from breweries is still illegal.

Brewpubs can now sell their beer in retail outlets. They can also produce a maximum of ten thousand barrels per year, versus the previous five thousand barrels per year. But if they do choose to distribute, they can't have taps from other breweries.

Breweries under 125,000 barrels of annual production can obtain a new Brewer Distributor permit, for a fee of $250, to self-distribute 40,000 barrels per year. Essentially, this law means it's easier for breweries to get launched, giving more choices for beer drinkers to enjoy.

However, with SB 639, brewers cannot sell the right to distribute their products to wholesalers, while wholesalers can sell those same rights to one another. In other words, a self-distributing brewery that wants to use a third-party distributor to sell beer to retailers won't be compensated by the distributor, but the distributor can immediately sell that business to another distributor.

"The idea that a statute designed specifically to deprive an entire class of Texas small business owners of the cash value of their businesses could pass is disheartening and reprehensible, and we cannot help but question the motives of anyone who would cast a vote in favor of, or in any way support, such a provision," Jester King brewers wrote in a statement in March, when it became clear SB 639 was a package deal with the other bills.

But as a whole, the beer bills were regarded as a victory for the two main groups that had pushed hard for the reform. For Open the Taps, the bills were the very reason the organization existed. The grassroots group has virtually no financial stake in the beer industry at all; the five board members simply love beer. The 501c6 nonprofit formed after the 2011 Texas legislative session ended without any of the reforms that Texas craft beer advocates had been hoping to see. Cofounder Leslie Sprague said that because the laws dictating restrictions for breweries and brewpubs were crafted in the 1930s, during Prohibition days, they need updating.

"How is it fair that breweries can't sell their own beers at their establishments?" she said. "The laws are bizarre. We're a group of consumers who want them to change to improve the craft beer experience for everyone."

When the 2013 Texas legislative session kicked off in January, Open the Taps was ready. Group members had hired a lobbyist firm, Cornerstone Government Affairs, and had met with lawmakers such as Senator John Carona of Dallas along with beer industry members and other groups, such as the guild, to lay out their interests and to educate the legislators (many of whom, she said, weren't even aware that breweries or brewpubs existed in their districts) on why the current laws aren't working.

For the most part, Sprague said, the legislators, such as State Senators Kevin Eltife and Leticia Van de Putte, were very open to changing the laws and hearing out their concerns until, about midway through the session, Carona—one of the key figures Sprague and others thought was on their side with a pro-business attitude—staged a coup with SB 639 that almost upset the progress they'd made. Because it was one in the set of bills getting passed, they had to accept it.

The Open the Taps founders live in Houston but came to Austin as often as they could, hosting events at area bars such as the Flying Saucer to spread the word and encourage people to call their respective legislators. The push obviously worked, but Sprague said there are yet more laws that could use some tweaking.

Just as instrumental, if not more so, was the guild.

Although Charles Valhonrat hasn't been the executive director of the guild for long, having gotten the post in October—the only position that's both appointed and paid—he's already noticed how capably Austin brewers work together. Their cooperation and collaboration not only means tireless work on getting the beer bills passed but also continues to mean they act as capable mentors for some of the brewers in Dallas and Houston who haven't been as neck deep in hops, malts and yeasts for nearly as long.

Valhonrat, a homebrewer from Houston who splits his time between there and Austin now for his guild job, notices the differences among the three

Rogness Brewing hosts concerts and game nights to encourage community building. This group is enjoying some Rogness beers while at a concert held at the brewery. *Caroline Wallace.*

Texas cities during the monthly guild meetings. In Austin, these meetings are more like casual gatherings at a local brewery in which attendees—mainly brewers, and sometimes others involved in the industry—drink a lot of beer and talk like old friends catching up (which pretty much sounds like the sort of meetings all offices should have).

"People like Tim [Schwartz of Real Ale] and Brian "Swifty" Peters [of Austin Beer Garden Brewing Co.] have done a great job of networking and updating their fellow brewers, so monthly meetings aren't as necessary as they used to be," Valhonrat said about the very social aspect to the Austin meet-ups.

Houston and Dallas have more educational gatherings, he said, with thirty-minute Q&As aimed at giving advice to new brewers.

"But I've noticed that Austin's deep sense of community is spreading to the other cities," he said. "They all want to know each other."

FROM THE ROCKIES TO THE HILL COUNTRY

At first, Joe Mohrfeld's decision to move from Colorado to Texas might not have made a lot of sense. Head brewer at the well-established and beloved Odell Brewing in Fort Collins, he wanted to open a brewpub in Austin with some friends, a place that would combine beer with one of its best edible accompaniments, pizza. The brewpub would carry more than forty local, regional and national beers on tap, in addition to the ones Mohrfeld would create himself. But why leave Colorado—a longtime bastion of craft beer—for Austin, where most of the breweries had not only opened within the past few years but were also too small to deliver their wares much past city limits?

Mohrfeld has an easy answer. He wants to help foster the community spirit that has made beer in Colorado more than just a tasty drink in a city he could see was already getting hooked on the IPAs and hefeweizens its own brewers concocted.

He's gotten his wish. The brewpub, Pinthouse Pizza, has become exactly the neighborhood gathering spot he intended it to be when he opened it in the fall of 2012. There, a mix of families and twenty-something beer drinkers gather around the long picnic-style tables that cover much of the open but cozy space. Mohrfeld still gets to brew beer. Now, he's also able to share his love of it more often with the patrons who line up for a pint in front of the tap wall, some unaware that *hop* isn't just a verb.

"We wanted to be the sort of spot that teaches everyone about craft beer, so we put out a very serious beer menu," he said, noting that, on a busy weekend, the more than forty guest taps can often have ten different beers rotating through by Sunday. But there isn't just one style of beer that the eclectic palates of serious beer drinkers in the city stick to; he's noticed patrons just as willing to try a variety of styles. That openness means brewers can experiment and find appreciative beer lovers eagerly waiting to discover what new sour they will tap next.

Moreover, Mohrfeld doesn't believe the flourishing business of microbreweries in Austin is a fad.

"We can become this great beer destination city, like Denver," he said. "But unlike Colorado, where the beer is shipped out to other states, people will have to come and see for themselves what Austin's beer scene is like."

That's because even the largest of Austin's breweries is still operating a system under ten thousand barrels, and many brewers prefer for their operations to stay small, with the goal of creating just enough beer for what they think is their market.

Christine Celis (daughter of Pierre Celis) pals around with Pinthouse Pizza brewer Joe Mohrfeld at the brewpub's first ever Belgian Beer Festival in May 2013. *Caroline Wallace.*

THE RELIGION BEHIND GOOD BEER

Any craft beer enthusiast who makes the rounds at local breweries, chances are, has at one point or another bumped elbows near the tap wall with Jake Maddux and his equally friendly wife, Monica.

Tall and bearded (as so many of the brewers and other male beer drinkers in Austin are), Maddux hasn't been brewing regularly since his days at Thirsty Planet, but he's got big plans and intends to open up a brewpub of his own soon that he'll call the Brewer's Table, a name at the heart of his philosophy toward beer. For Maddux, beer has, yes, a level of philosophical significance that other beverages simply can't muster. That's why he's the "Beer Evangelist" on Twitter—he wants to spread his passion for craft beer to anyone in desperate need of conversion (which, let's be honest, is pretty much anyone not drinking the stuff).

Brewing the drink isn't just a means to an end. Watching the looks of undoubtedly unbridled delight on people's faces as they try the Thirsty Planet Franklin Smoked Porter (a brew he had a hand in making) is sure part of the fun, but so is the actual brewing process itself. He calls it a Zen experience, finding a certain peace in the discovery that the more he learned, the less he knew.

An Oklahoma native, Maddux joined the U.S. Marine Corps Reserves at the age of seventeen and deployed to South America. He had a vastly different expectation for his life at that point, thinking he'd be a career officer. That didn't happen. Instead, he expanded his horizon in a much different manner. He worked at the alcoholic beverage–distributing company Glazer's, met Brian Smittle at the brewpub Smittle coowned in Oklahoma at the time, helped out a family friend at a Napa Valley winery (during which time he met Monica), worked at Anchor Brewing in San Francisco and temped at the Fort Collins brewery New Belgium for a year before Smittle lured him down to Austin to become his right-hand man at Thirsty Planet.

Many a Marine Corps veteran will say his service was among the most important and life-changing things he'd ever do, but for Maddux, hearing Smittle wax rhapsodic about beer was, too. Maddux said that was when brewing become a cult and a religion for him. It became even more so when he moved to Austin.

"You know, I've been all over, but this has been the most amazing beer community," he said. "It's young, and it's hungry. And we're the chosen few to the lead the second renaissance of craft beer in Austin."

And where Maddux goes, others will certainly follow. Voted by *Austin Beer Guide* editors as "the best personality" in Austin's craft beer scene, he could easily be confused as one of the brewers at Hops & Grain for how often he's there and how close he is to Josh Hare, Bob Galligan and other Hops & Grain guys, but he also frequents many of the other popular beer joints. Once he finds a spot in East Austin that fits his vision for a brewpub, he'll be there as well, crafting a rustic heaven of beer and food after learning so much from Smittle and Hare. Someday, his patrons might be tasting a "Semper Rye" with more looks of unbridled delight.

"I wanted something to believe in when I left the Marine Corps," he said. "I [discovered it] when I found the beer scene."

A "HI" POINT FOR CRAFT BEER

Like Mohrfeld, William Bearden—tasting room manager at Hops & Grain and former beer manager at East Austin pub Hi Hat Public House—became one of Austin craft beer's biggest proponents from an unlikely place. He worked in the cellar of the Duchman Family Winery in Driftwood during college. He managed a now-defunct wine pub called Fion for two and a half years. And he convinced his patrons at Cru Wine Bar to put down the house Sauvignon Blanc and try out Harpoon Pumpkin Ale.

By the time he was sneaking in extra beers to Cru's bar menu, he realized he'd chosen the wrong alcoholic beverage to make a job out of and wanted out. Not just out—he wanted a way into selling beer instead.

He had begun homebrewing four years before during his time at the winery, after one of his co-workers approached him and asked him if he wanted to brew beer with him once they'd clocked out. The offer stopped him cold for a moment.

"Brew beer?" he remembered asking. "Aren't we a winery?" But his co-worker explained that while his and many other wine industry workers' day jobs might have been all about grapes, their hobby was about hops and malts. It didn't take long for Bearden to understand why.

"For wine fans, I noticed over and over that all they cared about was how much their wine cost," he said. "Plus, to be a good winemaker, you have to take a step back, and let the wine make itself. Beer isn't like that—you can almost taste the brewers' hands in it."

Let's hope they washed them.

When Bearden found a Craigslist job posting for beer manager at a not-yet-opened pub on the east side, he applied, and owner Steve Shrader selected him

Left: Former Hi Hat Public House bar manager William Bearden pours a beer for a thirsty customer (this photographer). *Caroline Wallace.*

Opposite: Zoey Provino changes the beer menu at Hi Hat Public House. *Caroline Wallace.*

over almost four hundred other applicants to put together the beer list for Hi Hat Public House's twenty-four taps. Hi Hat opened in December 2012. Bearden ushered the beer bar through its early days before going to work in Hops & Grain's tasting room in July 2013, after the brewery was able to sell beer on site.

Bearden, who once went through a sommelier program to become an expert on wine, certainly knows his beer, too. When he was in charge of Hi Hat's beer list, on it was a variety of styles—from Thirsty Planet's Franklin Smoked Porter to Independence Brewing's Lupulust Tripel—that changed constantly so that regulars never got bored and newcomers always had something tasty to try. And these newcomers, he noticed, weren't exactly the stereotype for craft beer drinkers, a fact that he loves.

Because Hi Hat is tucked into the first floor of a building dedicated to housing low-income residents, it's gotten a variety of customers. Sometimes

an older lady with a cane walks in and downs a pint of Live Oak HefeWeizen as if it's water. And tough Hispanic guys—*vatos*, as Bearden called them—stroll in asking for Miller Lite. Bearden said that on one such occasion, he suggested they try Krombacher Pils and poured it to them in flute-shaped pilsner glasses, and now, they come in willing to fork out six bucks for "that beer with the special glass."

He appreciated seeing new faces in the pub because a growing community of people thirsting for craft beer, he believes, is the only way small breweries with big visions can continue to thrive and sell to bars like Hi Hat.

A bottle share at Hi Hat Public House is an excellent way to bring members of the beer community together. *Holly Aker.*

Bearden has some ideas about how these breweries, as well as craft beer–specialized spots like Hi Hat, continue drawing in legions of craft beer fans.

Events, he said, are crucial. During his Hi Hat days, he helped to plan every-other-month bottle shares, pint nights (in which dinner is tailored toward a certain beer) and deals such as Taco Tuesdays that get patrons a meal of two tacos and a beer for ten dollars. He said he brainstormed to continue coming up with events that, like the bottle share, conveyed the sense of community and camaraderie he's noticed exists in craft beer.

"I don't want to be thirty years old and saying I was there when the craft beer scene popped," he said. "I want to be thirty and have Austin be recognized as a craft beer mecca that people will go to, like Portland or Colorado, because they know it has great local beer."

Not that he has a problem with Portland's or Colorado's beer getting shipped to Austin. Hi Hat was one of the bars launching Firestone Walker when the California brewery's beer started arriving in Texas early in 2013. He actually thinks outside beers coming in are a boon to Austin.

"It'll light a fire under Texans to support our state," he said. "Competition in that way is good."

Lone Star State of Mind

With so many fantastic local options, others argue there's no reason to be shipping in beer from other states. Local blogger Matt Abendschein, founder of *You Stay Hoppy Austin*, even offers a challenge asking that for one month, people pledge to drink only Texas brews. For the month of June for the third consecutive year, that's what he and some of his blog followers did, before throwing a big bash at, appropriately enough, Craft Pride, the only bar in Austin built around the concept of exclusively offering Texas taps.

He explained the reason why the local-only mindset is so important. Not because Texans or Austinites are being the self-important snobs who believe our state is better than the others (even though it is, obviously) but because this sort of thinking inspires community.

"As big as Austin gets, it still has this small communal vibe where people really seem to grasp the concept of supporting local, independent businesses," he said. "In Austin, you feel like you're part of something."

And isn't it cool, he said, to see the fifty-four taps on Craft Pride's wall and know they're all from Texas?

That might have been tricky to do even two years ago, but it's no problem now. The founders of the Rainey Street bar, JT and Brandy Egli, can choose beers from twenty-five very busy breweries, all ones that Craft Pride works with, to fill the tap wall, as well as two rotating cask engines.

The husband and wife had been homebrewers—Brandy had picked up a trick or two from her cousin, Forrest Rogness, who owns Austin Homebrew Supply and Rogness Brewing—when they decided to invest all they had in a bit of property in one of Austin's thriving nightlife districts, a series of bungalows-turned-bars just south of downtown. They knew they wanted the bar to serve up Texas beers only, a risk that has so far paid off since they opened Craft Pride in February 2013.

The couple really does take pride in their project. It's not just about the beer. The building itself is an homage to Texas craftsmanship, with all the tables and the bar top made from the same tree, a live oak that had towered in an area about an hour north from the bar. All of the wood—even beer flights come in blocks carved to look like miniature tree trunks—creates a homey atmosphere, a place where beer lovers can seek refuge from the liquor-swigging partiers that often crowd Rainey Street.

Helping the Eglis, a couple who had no prior industry experience before Craft Pride, was "beer guru" Chris Booth. He had a hand in opening brewpub Black Star Co-op and Rainey Street's other popular beer spot,

Fish Fry Bingo, aka the official band of Texas craft beer, performs during the Big Texas Beer Festival in Dallas. *Caroline Wallace.*

Banger's Sausage House and Beer Garden, before the Eglis hired him to take charge of the beer menu.

"This has been a great fit," he said in May 2013, before he departed Craft Pride's staff. "I like the husband-and-wife team behind it. We've had the same values, same vision. We want to represent Texas craft beer."

But they certainly won't spit out a swill of an out-of-state lager. For more options, in case the tap wall just won't do it, there's also a bottle shop that carries bombers of both local and national offerings. It's underutilized, Booth said, although that could change as more people learn about Craft Pride.

Events such as Abendschein's June State Beer Challenge Celebration could draw the crowds, as could continued beer-and-food pairings from the Bacon Bus and any other food trucks that are planted in Craft Pride's courtyard. These kinds of pairings, beer with food, are the next frontier, Booth said, one of the best ways to draw in beer novices. During May's American Craft Beer Week, for example, Craft Pride made sure the beer specials all came with a side of bacon.

A Hoppy Man

The premise is pretty simple, albeit alliterative: a boat, some bats and lots of beers. Abendschein, aka *You Stay Hoppy Austin*, has turned the "Bats & Beer" event into a classic Austin party. He's partnered with Capital Cruises for more than a half dozen of the Lady Bird Lake boat tours, an evening during which special casks are tapped and quickly slurped down and not much bat-seeing goes on.

Watching the Mexican free-tailed bats blacken the horizon as they take off into the night from the Congress Avenue bridge (normally a very popular tourist attraction) isn't exactly the main point of Bats & Beers anyway. Abendschein just wants all the boat guests to have a good time and taste some good beer in the process.

He's been blogging for almost three years and has earned the respect of Austin's beer community, drumming up about ten thousand page views each month, a number far beyond what he expected when he first started out. That respect might have a little to do with the fact that he can name his favorite beers in about one minute flat, and they're all locally produced. (Austin Beerworks's Einhorn, a citrusy Berliner weisse that has locals salivating for summer, is at the top of the list, followed closely behind by just about any brew Jester King's made.)

Remember, he's big into the go-local movement when it comes to beer and urges others to be, too.

"We get excited about beers coming in from other states and forget how good we have it with the local stuff," he said. Plus, he doesn't see any of it going away anytime soon, as long as Austin brewers maintain the same good-natured, noncompetitive attitude they've always had.

"There's that underlying business model, yeah. You have to make money, set yourself apart," Abendschein said. "But at the same time, you're out to help each other, promote each other; you see a lot of places here giving equipment away. Like Adelbert's, when they opened, the guys at Real Ale were saying, 'Watch out for this, that, do this'—they were able to open up that much faster because of the advice, all the little things you should know about fixing up a building."

On *You Stay Hoppy Austin*, the blog is divided into several sections. The tab on Austin breweries offers his reviews on specific beers, and a calendar keeps up a pretty comprehensive list of all the beer-related to-dos going on around town. He also has a series of interviews he's done with local brewers that he calls "For the Love of Craft Beer." It's a Q&A-style post in which he asks

Bromance blooms between *You Stay Hoppy Austin*'s Matt Abendschein (center) and Carlos Arrellano (left) and with Adan De La Torre (right) of CaskATX at Thirsty Planet's third-anniversary party. *Caroline Wallace.*

guys like Ron Extract with Jester King and Josh Hare with Hops & Grain why they like beer so much. He said his "rants" section, his own humorous take on ridiculous beer-related news, is pretty popular, although sometimes people take them a little too seriously.

They shouldn't, he said. Like drinking beer, his blog is all in good fun.

ABG: AWFUL BOOZY GUYS

Brewmor: The *Austin Beer Guide* dudes were originally supposed to write this book but were too busy procreating to bother.

That's the sort of gentle ribbing, grounded in a grain of truth, that readers of the seasonal guide might find tucked in with a variety of feature pieces, brewery lists and photos chronicling the Austin beer scene. The brewmor section (*brew* plus *rumor*—get it?) is all in good fun and not hard fact, but the four guys behind the guide must now include a disclaimer at the beginning of the brewmors that makes it clear a brewmor is "a beer related story or statement in general circulation without confirmation or certainty as to facts."

"There's always someone who takes offense, so we try to include people we know can take it," Chris Troutman, one of the ABG cofounders, said. (Note: we should know: *Bitch Beer* has been featured twice.)

The side project of four beer-lovin' dudes—Troutman, Aaron Chamberlain, Josh Spradling and Shawn Phillips—was first published in the spring of 2011 and was then a small thirty-page guide that consisted mainly of brewery and brewpub profiles. They distributed the first edition during South by Southwest, Austin's massive music, film and interactive festival, after printing only one thousand copies.

By comparison, the Summer 2013 issue of *Austin Beer Guide* is a robust eighty-eight-page magazine, its 8,500 copies circulating around the city's local bars, restaurants and other random venues. It's a pretty good bet that if you see some, one of the ABG guys has probably been there. It's an even better bet that he probably had a beer while there.

Like the magazine, the craft beer scene in Austin has changed a lot in the two interim years since ABG launched. It's not just that there are more breweries now. There are also more bloggers and writers clamoring to cover every last drop of brew. "Beer media" back then, they noticed, was primarily the *Austin American-Statesman* (the Texas capital city's main daily newspaper) and the *Austin Chronicle*, and neither of these publications covered beer exclusively.

Chamberlain's and Troutman's respective blogs, however, did. In the few years before ABG, there was Chamberlain's blog, Craft Austin, and Troutman's blog, Beer Town Austin, which he worked on with his brother-in-law and his friend Shawn Phillips, now ABG's photographer.

"Aaron was really good at saying, 'This is happening now' and would have eight posts a day. Events coming up, new beers coming out, that kind of thing," Troutman said. "Whereas...the three of us were doing Beer Town and we'd do more video interviews. We would do more long-form stuff. Maybe once a week at the most."

They eventually decided to combine their strengths—Chamberlain handles production at *Texas Monthly*—after noticing each other at beer events. At first, they simply produced podcasts together. But beer so often inspires bright ideas, and in 2010, they discussed collaborating on a more ambitious project, the guide. By that point, Spradling had come on board.

It was immediately obvious, though, that a lot more sweat, planning and late-night drinking would be required to print a magazine than to put out a blog. Because of their backgrounds in publishing and writing, they knew what a full-scale magazine would take and didn't want to produce a subpar product.

"We knew if it was going to be anything decent then we'd have to sell ads," Troutman said. "We shelved the idea at first."

Selling ads didn't turn out to be the big burden they had originally thought; many of the breweries and brewpubs they reached out to already knew who they were and readily forked over the money they needed to fund the crisp white booklet into existence.

With two years passed and ten issues published, the ABG guys are as knowledgeable about the local craft breweries as the brewers themselves are, and they've noticed some trends. For one, they've seen Austin slowly start to resemble Fort Collins, Colorado, another beer town, much more than it used to. Troutman and Chamberlain credit the transformation to Jester King, the first brewery "that made a culture out of going to a brewery to drink every weekend," Troutman said.

It didn't used to be that way. When a brewery threw an anniversary party or other event, such as Independence's First Saturday tours, they were "big deals" that could be hard to get into because everyone wanted tickets and the chance to kick back with the brewers who crafted their favorite beers. The events lasted a few hours, and then they were gone.

"It's never been where you can say, 'What do you want to do this weekend?'" Troutman said. "'Oh, let's go to the brewery and get drunk.' And you have Friday options, Saturday options, Sunday options. Hops & Grain is almost a bar to go to after work on Fridays."

With the recent laws now blurring once clear lines among Texas breweries, bars and brewpubs, Troutman thinks going to a brewery is already becoming less of a to-do and more of a casual opportunity to hang out, the sort of activity that you might find in Fort Collins, another college town.

"It has a bunch of brewpubs, breweries and bars, and you can hop on a bike and pop in, an hour at a brewery, an hour at a bar," he said. "We would go into one bar and meet guys from different breweries. That's like here. I think I see Bay [Anthon], the owner of Hopfields, at Draught House more than Hopfields."

His and Chamberlain's other, way more tongue-in-cheek, prediction that ABG will decide the future of Austin's craft beer ("Breweries are going to plan seasonals around release dates of new guides, and bars are looking at our maps and seeing where they can open," Chamberlain cracked) might be less accurate and more wishful thinking. Or, what do they call it? Oh, yeah. A brewmor.

THE BEST OF THE FESTS

The Texas Craft Brewers Festival is no different from any Austin festival worth its salt. Austinites and out-of-towners alike have turned the city into a destination for no-holds-barred entertainment extravaganzas, with Austin City Limits Festival and South by Southwest the two powerhouse festivals that put Austin on the map for music, interactive technology and film lovers across the United States and the world.

There are tons of smaller festivals year-round for just about anything you can possibly think of (stand-up comedy, African-American book authors, international poetry and so forth), and the big one for beer, a collaborative effort of the Texas Craft Brewers Guild and social service organization the Young Men's Business League, is worth every penny of the twenty-dollar ticket. Plus, hey, it's for a good cause. All those pennies go toward the Austin Sunshine Camps, a nonprofit that helps underprivileged kids.

Like ACL and SXSW, the earlier founders of the Texas Craft Brewers Festival didn't quite realize the draw of what they were offering, but its allure quickly wised them up to making it the best possible celebration of beer it could be.

In its earliest incarnation, the festival was simply a project that Brian "Swifty" Peters pulled off in his Bitter End days, when Austin had little more than brewpubs and a couple of craft breweries to its name. After he stopped, the street in front of Bitter End remained clear of festival booths and kegs for a few years until Amy Cartwright of Independence Brewing Company, who had worked at the brewpub until 1998, brought the fest back to life with her husband, Rob.

They carried the torch of festival coordination for three years. But once the couple was at work showing Austin that Independence could run with the big boys of Real Ale and Live Oak, the Texas Craft Brewers Festival again became a booze-filled memory.

Its most recent rebirth was through the careful direction of the Texas Craft Brewers Guild a few years ago, and it's become one of the most sure-fire ways to introduce craft beer novices to the variety of breweries that Texas has to offer, as well as one more fun opportunity for brewers to mingle with some of their biggest supporters and friends.

Guild director Charles Valhonrat projected that up to six thousand people would flood Fiesta Gardens, a sprawling outdoor space that overlooks Lady Bird Lake, for the September 28, 2013 festival, where forty breweries and

Crowds of beer fans gather at the 2012 Texas Craft Brewers Festival. *Holly Aker.*

Texas breweries serve beer at the 2012 Texas Craft Brewers Festival. *Holly Aker.*

brewpubs from Austin, Dallas, Fort Worth, Houston and San Antonio offered four ounce pours of their beers to the thirsty masses.

(The June beer legislation may have given Austin beer its biggest heyday yet, but one rule that hasn't changed is those pesky four-ounce pours. The Texas Alcoholic Beverage Commission won't allow an ounce more at public beer events like the festival—a drawback Valhonrat said is for another legislative session.)

Compare those attendance numbers to 2002, when the festival was under the Cartwrights' helm. That first year—with the Bitter End, Lovejoys, North by Northwest, Live Oak and Real Ale all featured—far exceeded their expectations.

"The festival before we took it on was small enough to utilize street closures," Amy said. "So we did that, too, but the population base that wanted [the festival] was vastly bigger. We thought we'd be lucky if 1,500 people showed up. Instead, we sold out of everything, and the street closure in front of Bitter End wasn't big enough by a long shot."

They tried to move the event to a park, but the Austin Parks and Recreation Department was a little skittish.

"I guess back then, they didn't really understand the sort of people that drink craft beer," Amy said with a laugh. "They had it in their mind that all these really drunk people would descend on the streets of Austin. We had to explain our crowd, but they still asked some strange questions. 'How are you going to make sure people don't show up drunk? How can you be sure they won't bring in outside booze?' It was a little bizarre."

So instead, the remaining two festivals the Cartwrights were in charge of took place in a parking lot. Amy said it didn't feel right to take on any more because by the time their third festival had rolled around, Independence was up and running. To her, owning a brewery and producing a craft beer festival felt like a conflict of interest, a possible leg up on the other breweries.

She said the Texas Craft Brewers Festival is rightfully the responsibility of the guild and the Young Men's Business League, with all breweries involved pitching in.

"With the guild, there's structure and so much more community," she said.

CHAPTER EIGHT
ONWARD, UPWARD

PAIRS WITH ABGB'S BIG MAMA RED

With each passing day, Austin is gaining more and more transplants. Mirroring the continuing swell of the city, Austin's beer scene continues to grow. Following the craft beer boom of 2012, the coming years promise to bring rapid expansion. Older breweries are growing their walls outward, and new breweries are popping up faster and faster. As the audience for craft beer grows, so does the demand for new and inventive brews. In a creative environment like Austin, there will always be passionate people gearing up to open the next great brewery. As the future is no longer the future as soon as it happens, it is important to note that this chapter is accurate as of July 2013. We can in no way promise that every brewery mentioned in this chapter will make it, nor can we ensure that the information will not evolve as these breweries firm up their investors and plans for the future. Grab your imperial red and toast to the future of Austin beer.

SCORE ONE FOR AUSTIN'S BREWERIES

Literally as we wrote this book, the landscape and scope of the beer scene in Austin was changing. With the passing of recent beer laws, breweries are poised to change to new permits and overwhelmingly increase their profits. As explained in chapter seven, the Texas government recently passed beer laws that will allow breweries to sell to consumers on site. This is a huge

Landmark beer legislation passed in 2013 now grants new rights for breweries and brewpubs in Texas. *Caroline Wallace.*

change in comparison to the former beer laws, which had not changed since Prohibition, with the exception of the brewpub laws in the '90s. Now that Governor Rick "Good Hair" Perry has signed the bills into effect, the city is gearing up for a new day in Austin beer.

Because these new laws are in place, many craft breweries are faced with the decision of whether or not to switch permits. In many other states, brewpubs and craft breweries are more or less legally synonymous. In Texas, there has always been a necessary divide between brewpubs and breweries because of the state's laws. With the modifications enacted by CSSB 515-518 and 639 outlined in the previous chapter, brewpubs and breweries are becoming more similar legally than ever, although there are still some key differences. Organizations such as Open the Taps continue to advocate and will not give up until production breweries are allowed to send their taproom visitors home with a six-pack or growler.

We hope the changes in the beer laws will mean that the breweries in Austin will follow the rest of the country's lead and start to curate craft beer taprooms that feel more like neighborhood bars. One day, we may

Black Star Co-op brewer Jeff Young fills growlers with his beers so patrons can take them to go. *Suzy Schaffer.*

see fewer warehouse-style breweries and more beautiful (air-conditioned) taprooms that are fabulous year-round. Many are already starting to extend their hours.

WIDE OPEN SPACES

Now that the game has changed, older breweries are looking to expand, open new locations and reclassify as brewpubs. So far Hops & Grain, Infamous and Jester King have all filed for brewpub status. For smaller breweries, this is a good option because they are able to sell beer to go as well as from their taprooms. Unfortunately, if brewpubs choose to self-distribute, they can no longer have guest brews on their tap walls. Though not ideal, brewpubs will have to make the hard choice between guest taps and selling beer off-site. Either way, we should start to see shelves lined with beer from brewpubs around the state as the crowd demands, "More beer!" from these Austin staples, and we look forward to the changes they have in store.

Live Oak Brewing Company

Live Oak Brewing has been an Austin staple since it opened its doors in 1997. Making beautiful beers that patrons can drink all day with little issue for palate or tolerance, Live Oak has thus far offered its beers only on draft. As it looks to the future and toward expansion, Live Oak finally plans to add a canning line. This means that we will eventually get to buy Live Oak HefeWeizen off a grocery shelf. Live Oak has bought a piece of land in Southeast Austin that it plans to use to expand the brewery. Affectionately referred to as "the Mullet" by Chip McElroy, the new brewery site will be business in the front and party in the back. Surrounded by live oak trees, the new facility will be twenty thousand square feet, a large improvement on the current eight-thousand-square-foot warehouse in East Austin. There are even rumors that the river surrounding the brewery will be used to ferry people around.

Real Ale Brewing Company

In a 2013 panel discussion at the Austin Food and Wine Festival, Real Ale owner Brad Farbstein admitted that with the brewery's new expanded real estate, a distillery is in Real Ale's future. Following the example set by San Antonio's Ranger Creek, Blanco will soon have its own brewstillery. Self-barrel aging is bound to be in its future.

In the meantime, Real Ale has bought up several thousand feet's worth of space that it plans on using to expand. There would be plenty of room to hold a monster canning line, which would make sense given that it has almost outgrown its current one. We do know that Real Ale will use the added space to create a top-notch new tasting area, devoid of the need for any safety glasses. This should benefit the consumer, who will hopefully start

Real Ale has been focusing on expanding its barrel program. *Holly Aker.*

to find more delicious canned beer coming from Real Ale, as well as create a new on-site experience out in Blanco.

Pierre Celis Brewery

As recounted in chapter three, the story of Celis Brewery is not only one of world-renowned beer but also one that transcends continents, corporations and generations. After Miller Brewing Company sold the Celis name, equipment and recipes to Michigan Brewing Company in 2002, Christine Celis promised her aging father, Pierre, that she would not rest until she had recovered the family name. Unfortunately, Pierre would not live to see the day come, but Christine did fulfill that oath.

In June 2012, Michigan Brewing Company, which filed for Chapter Seven bankruptcy a few months earlier, sold its remaining assets at auction to satisfy its debts. Among these assets was the Celis trademark.

"It has been my personal dream and passion to carry on my father's legacy," Christine said in a press release after the auction. "After his death...we stepped up the intensity of our plans for a new brewery and re-acquiring the family name was the one thing we really needed to begin moving forward."

Christine, who has remained an Austinite and even traded in her green card for official American citizenship a few years ago, now plans to bring her father's recipes back to the capital city. The new brewery will be known as Pierre Celis Brewery so there's no confusing it with the reincarnations of Celis beers brewed under Miller and Michigan Brewing Company.

For Christine, the prospect of paying homage to her father is just as important as her quest to reintroduce the original Celis White recipe, which has never really been available in its original glory after Miller pressured the brewery to make it taste more commercially viable in the mid-1990s.

"I want to brew the witbier that started it all," Christine said. "I want to continue his legacy. He did way too much for the brewing industry not to. He was one of those pioneers."

In an act of kismet that's equal parts splendid and sorrowful, Christine now finds herself in a very similar position to where her father was more than fifty years earlier in that pub in Hoegaarden, holding the key to resurrecting the authentic, traditional Hoegaarden witbier. Just as Pierre revived the style after a decade lost, so too will Christine, after nearly two. While the core of Pierre Celis Brewery will be those classic recipes, Christine also plans to add some over-the-top, experimental creations of her own.

While the plans for Pierre Celis Brewery are not completely finite at the time of this writing, Christine said she was planning to start with a collaboration beer with a local Austin brewery before building her own facility. However, she is not in a rush to expand as rapidly as Celis, or for that matter Hoegaarden, did.

"This is a family brewery," Christine said. "I'm not looking to sell millions of barrels. I just want to have a small brewery and make beer that is always a consistent, high quality product. That's what my dad was known for and that's what I want to do."

In keeping with that family theme, several of the original employees of Celis Brewery will be returning to the new operation, including eighty-year-old brewing engineer and former employee Jean Luc Suys, who will be helping Christine get things off the ground.

"They want to work on the legacy of my dad because they had such a great experience working at Celis Brewery and they had a great relationship with my dad," Christine said.

On top of the involvement from original employees, Christine plans to literally keep it in the family, as her own daughter, Daytona, will actually be involved with the brewery, but first, Christine is sending her to Belgium for a year to connect with her heritage and study under Belgian brewmasters.

Now, Christine needs only to get the doors open and the kettles a-brewin'. "I can't wait to be up and running," Christine said. "It gives me a second chance. Many times in life, you never get a second chance."

COMING SOON TO A NEIGHBORHOOD NEAR YOU

Writing about the future of Austin beer is a tricky endeavor, as it is ever evolving and changing. As we pointed out in the chapter introduction, the information below is from interviews conducted in May and June 2013. As of now, there are many breweries at various stages in the launching process. We wish them all the best as they duke it out to become the next best thing in Austin beer.

Austin Beer Garden Brewing Co. (ABGB)

Brainchild of high school friends Mark Jensen, Amos Lowe and couple Curtis and Jill Knobloch, Austin Beer Garden Brewing Co. will open in the summer of 2013. Joining this passionate team of beer lovers is Brian "Swifty" Peters, who chose to forgo his own project to stick with colleague and former Uncle Billy's brethren Amos Lowe. These two make a killer brewing team, taking gold in the Kellerbier category at the 2012 Great American Beer Festival for Uncle Billy's with their Bottle Rocket. The group believes that its beer is expected to knock people on their asses.

Working in its converted warehouse just off the heart of South Lamar, this brewery dream team is striving to create an "Austin in 1972" atmosphere with its retro feel.

"For a lot of things we ask ourselves, what would 1972 Austin do?" ABGB cofounder Mark Jensen said.

Austin Beer Garden Brewing Co. wants its customers to feel like the brewpub has always been there.

"The ABGB is sort of the call letter for that. I sort of wanted it to be a content generator so that it feels like a station," Jensen said. "There's a beer content to our station and a music content to our station, and there's a community content."

ABGB's Amos Lowe (left) and Mark Jensen (right) pose in front of their newly installed tanks. *Shaun Martin.*

Butcher paper covered the windows of ABGB in the months before the brewpub's opening. *Shaun Martin.*

The ABGB houses a fifteen-barrel system with nine serving tanks and the ability to brew lagers with a canning line on the way. Inside ABGB's refurbished party warehouse will be a long bar (complete with purse hooks and charging stations [#GoodOneGuys]), long family-style tables and a full stage. Also included will be two dartboards and two foosball tables, not to mention the locally sourced menu of tasty bar food. Outside will be a large cascading patio area, complete with reclaimed metal tables. ABGB's beer selection will include Lowe's and Peters's best versions of ten traditional styles. Not that they will be limited to that, of course, but ten mainstays is not a bad place to start.

4th Tap Brewing Co-op

In recent years, Austin has seen an influx of cooperatives such as Wheatsville Co-op and Black Star Co-op. Soon, 4th Tap Brewing Co-op will join the ranks. While many co-ops are member owned, 4th Tap plans on being worker owned. This plan will put them in the category with New Belgium and Full Sail as being one of the first worker-owned breweries in the country.

"A work-owned cooperative is owned by all the people that work for the cooperative...it's built so that they have decision-making power," 4th Tap cofounder John Stecker said.

John Stecker, Dariush Griffin and the rest of the crew from 4th Tap Brewing have been working closely with Black Star Co-op, hoping to gain knowledge on the structure of brewery co-ops.

"Chris is going to be our head brewer. He is the assistant brewer at [Black Star Co-op]," Stecker said.

The difference between the two is that 4th Tap will be a production brewery and will be worker owned instead of member owned. As members of cooperatives in town, they are also working with Cooperation Texas, a cooperative incubator, to help set up the co-op.

Known as the "wedding brewers," the men of 4th Tap began by homebrewing for their own wedding celebrations, as well as those of their friends.

"We started brewing for weddings, then more weddings, then events and then more parties," Stecker said. " And we started getting requests. So we kind of started following the wave."

In the last few years, this passionate group of friends took its penchant for homebrewing and decided to go into business. The co-op's setup currently consists of a fifty-gallon, all-grain system. It hopes to expand that quickly to a much larger system in North Austin. As the beer laws now allow for on-site beer sales, 4th Tap will have extended hours and taproom specials. The co-op wants to create a model that inspires community and does not compete with the bars that sell its beer.

The name 4th Tap was inspired by the brewers' passion for seasonals. As most traditional taprooms have three mainstays, the fourth tap is generally reserved for a small batch or rotating beer. The brewery will focus on interesting and unique styles that are as nontraditional as they are flavorful. As Stecker has a background in cell biology, 4th Tap will also have its very own brew lab. There is nothing like it in the state of Texas, and it will allow the group to cultivate its own yeast strains. 4th Tap expects to open sometime in 2014.

Bush Baby Beer

Tucked away off Airport Boulevard lies Bush Baby Beer. Part of a series of buildings on one sizeable property, it is an outdoor brewhouse where temperatures can rise up to 120 degrees when the wok burners (used as their heat source for brewing) are on full blast. This little patio addition is the site of all the brewing done by Bush Baby Beer. On the hottest day of 2012, twenty-five close family members and friends gathered to help the Yiapan family build the add-on that now houses its brewing system. It serves as a home for the brew equipment that has been laid out to be a near perfect miniature of a full production brewery. Bush Baby has been hard at work perfecting recipes that it hopes will translate quickly at a larger scale.

"We built a system that mimics a big brewery. A lot of the trouble when you make that transition from small to big is that all these recipes that you work on...the smaller system is just not accurate," Bush Baby brewer Aoibhistin Cooney said.

Run by Brio, Benjamin and Mushahidi Yiapan and Aoibhistin Cooney, Bush Baby Beer will not be your typical production brewery. While it will still be looking to make a profit from its wares, a large sum of its income will be donated to help build water wells in Africa. Another sizeable donation will be made to the local Austin community.

As a young man in Kenya, Brio's father, Mushahidi Ole Yiapan, brewed beer from honey and corn with his father. Later on in life, Yiapan was shot

Bush Baby Beer brews on its pilot system in a lush outdoor space in Austin. *Shaun Martin.*

Bush Baby Beer founder Brio Yiapan's father, Mushahidi Ole Yiapan (striped shirt in center), was a brewer in Kenya before he immigrated to the United States. *Courtesy of Bush Baby Beer.*

A vintage beer sign will soon be installed at Austin Beer Garden Brewing Co.. *Shaun Martin.*

during the Kenyan war for independence while being held in a prison camp. Fortunately, he was taken to a Catholic mission to heal where he received a full education. Soon after completing his schooling, he went to work for the Tusker Brewing Company, which sent him to Scotland to learn the technique of brewing.

"Dad grew up in Kenya in a mud hut and ended up raising to the rank of brewer in the main brewery in Kenya, Tusker Brewing," Benjamin Yiapan said.

He returned to Kenya to work as a brewer until moving to the States after falling in love with an American traveler.

As a young adult, Brio returned to Kenya and was inspired by the people and circumstances she encountered to start a charity called Well Aware, which builds clean water wells in Africa. After growing tired of constantly trying to find funding, the family decided that they needed a way to donate to the cause consistently. As a longtime philanthropist, Brio was inspired by her father's background in brewing. Bush Baby Beer was born out of the combination of philanthropy and brewing history.

"The main drive will be in Africa, but some unknown percentage will be donated locally," Cooney said. "And then some group of people, maybe people who are members or people who purchase our beer or something, will decide then what to do with the local funds."

Bush Baby Beer is still looking for a space to launch its production brewery but hopes to find one that facilitates community and outreach.

"We are planning on opening with a fifteen-barrel system…Realistically we are looking at a year to a year and a half before we are on the shelf," Brio said.

Bush Baby will brew more simple styles that are sessionable and built for Texas's hot temperatures. It hopes to inspire people and make good beer at the same time.

Good Libations Brewing Company

Two old friends open a brewery. While it's a common tale, Andy Rinehart and Tim Albright from Good Libations have been working toward opening their brewery for more than a decade. Well, we should say Albright has been trying to get Rinehart onboard for more than a decade, and his efforts are finally coming to fruition. Good Libations will be opening in the next year or two and will feature mainstay beers that cross all four seasons. As the name implies, Good Libations will focus on "good people, good times and good beer."

Currently brewing out of a house in North Austin, Good Libations is perfecting as many of its recipes and processes as it can on its homebrew system. From makeshift brew lab to kegerator, Good Libations is already on its way to brewing great beer. Rinehart and Albright have been working to mimic the entire brewing process in their own backyard.

"We're dialing in all of the processes that we can," Rinehart said.

Though they have a pretty sweet setup, Good Libations is hoping to open a full production brewery complete with an enticing taproom and a flavorful beer selection. They are looking to set up more than just a warehouse space. Rinehart and Albright want to create a place where people want to come and hang out.

While Albright had the idea for the brewery and has been a homebrewer for a long time, Rinehart has been skeptical until recently.

"Tim's been brewing for like seventeen years, and I have been brewing for about five," Rinehart said.

For the last few years, Rinehart has been working for breweries in town to learn the production side of brewing as well as making beer. Rinehart believes that he and Albright balance each other out, one preferring hoppier flavors and the other preferring maltier flavors. An admitted control freak, Rinehart will be perfecting recipes until the brewery's opening.

Guns & Oil Brewing Co.

Brewing "beer for the bold," Guns & Oil hopes to bring out the cowboy in everyone. Currently, Guns & Oil is going through permit issues that have held up its grand opening. Originally scheduled to launch in May 2013, Guns & Oil is working toward opening late in the summer of 2013.

"We are damn close to launching, and I can't wait. I am sick of talking about beer and can't wait to be selling it," Cary Prewitt, founder of Guns & Oil said.

Taking a slightly different approach to opening a brewery, Guns & Oil is currently contract brewing out of a friend's brewing facility in New Mexico, with plans to open a brewery in Austin after perfecting the product. As with most endeavors, Guns & Oil is still seeking out investors to begin to set up its physical location. Rather than going all in all at once, Prewitt is brewing on a borrowed system.

"For now this makes the most sense because we can start the brewery, sell beer and prove [the] model," Prewitt said.

While this allows less control in the initial processes, it is cost effective and will allow Guns & Oil to open more quickly in Austin.

Guns & Oil will launch with a lager just in time for the end of Austin's sweltering summer and will add more styles as it grows. Prewitt explained that he wants to brew beer that people want to drink more than once.

"Our beers are not going to be as craft as a Firemans #4 per se," Prewitt said.

Guns & Oil will focus on traditional, sessionable styles and hopes to build a fan base of craft beer drinkers and non–craft beer drinkers alike.

Zilker Brewing Co.

Named after one of Austin's most iconic landmarks, Zilker Brewing hopes to become just as much of a household name as its namesake city park. While not all its beers are named after Austin landmarks, you should start to see the likes of Greenbelt on the grocery shelves as early as the end of 2013. The men of Zilker Brewing, Forrest and Patrick Clark and Marco Rodriguez, have been homebrewing together for five years and have been actively working on the brewery as a business concept for the last two.

The Clark brothers and Rodriguez are mostly self-taught homebrewers with a dream of opening a brewery with a community focus and accessible, sessionable beer. The goal for Zilker is to keep the beers light and flavorful.

Cofounders of Zilker Brewing Company (from left to right) Patrick Clark, Forrest Clark and Marco Rodriguez brew test batches on their ten-gallon system. *Shaun Martin.*

"We brew an American-Belgo style for the most part, which is kind of a hybrid between American-style beers and then we use a Belgian style yeast with American hops," Forrest said.

American-Belgo styles, while delicious, are also more rare, and Zilker hopes this will set them apart as they go to market. As with most opening breweries, the change in beer laws will help solidify Zilker's business plan up front, as it is able to sell beer directly from its taproom.

Currently brewing out of one of the founder's garages on a ten-gallon system, Zilker plans on going to a full system as soon as permits and location searches allow.

Many new breweries are having issues with finding locations to brew as only certain areas are permitted for it, and there are only so many warehouses in Austin. Developers and brewers are currently at war for land.

"The warehouse space is really competitive over [in East Austin]," Forrest said. "We actually had a site plan going on in an East Side warehouse and then a developer came and bought up the whole property."

This means higher rent and less availability for new brewers to find something within the city limits. The Zilker men are looking for a space in town (a much cherished location) but hope to find a space large enough to fit all their needs.

Community is important to the Zilker Brewing model, and it hopes to build a space for collaboration and experimentation.

"We also want to team with other local businesses," Forrest said. "We have already done an art gallery grand opening, gave them some beer. So you can see more partnerships there, maybe having art on display at [the brewery]."

Zilker wants to make beers that can be enjoyed by both craft beer aficionados and average beer drinkers alike.

Orf Brewing

Chris Orf has been aspiring toward opening Orf Brewing since he moved to Austin in 2006. With a background in improv and sketch comedy, his goal is to "bring the fun" however he can. Growing up in St. Louis, Orf was exposed only to the traditional American light lagers.

"I was born and raised in St. Louis, where your varieties were Budweiser, Busch or, if you wanted to get fancy, Michelob," Orf said.

After going to college in Portland, Oregon, his love for craft beer was ignited. Learning that there were more beers out there than Bud Light, Orf began homebrewing and putting his chemistry degree to good work.

Chris Orf has been striving toward his dream of opening a brewery since 2006. *Shaun Martin.*

Orf began brewing in the mid-1990s and began to concept out a brewpub and comedy theater while working in comedy on the East Coast. After moving to Austin for love, Orf realized that land was plentiful and breweries were few. At the time that he moved to Austin in 2006, there were only three major breweries open, though the likes of (512) and Jester King were in the works.

"Unfortunately I did things in kind of reverse order. I had the wife and had the kid before I started the business," Orf said.

Now that his child is old enough, Orf is pursuing brewing with more vigor than ever.

Orf Brewing is currently running on a ten-gallon system and just purchased a fifty-gallon system. Following the likes of Twisted X, Orf plans to start small to "prove concept" and then quickly expand once his model has solidified. Bringing comedy and beer together, Chris wants to do improv shows during tours as well as sponsor comedy events.

"I like to provide the source of fun. Beer is one good source of fun, and I can do the comedy at the same time," Orf said.

Orf Brewing plans to brew off style and experimental beers. One of his flagships will be a honey-roasted black lager that reflects this concept. Honey is typically used in lighter beers, but Orf will be mixing it with the more complex black lager style.

"I don't make an IPA because everybody makes an IPA. But I do like an Irish red with the caramel maltiness, so I thought, 'What if I hop that up and strengthen it like an India pale ale would be, but it's an India red ale,'" Orf said.

Orf plans to entertain the Austin beer drinkers sometime in the next year or two.

Other Rumored Breweries

The following breweries were not available for interviews before the publishing of this book. As the life of a new brewer is hectic, we will not fault them for it. Opening a new brewery is a lot like giving birth (we imagine, on both counts). Therefore, labor pains include a busy schedule and a low-budget website. Please excuse our lack of info, but we still thought these new guys were worth mentioning.

Black & Red Brewing Co.

While not much is known about Black & Red Brewing Co., its main mission statement is local ingredients and sustainability. It is still in the startup phase but has announced a King Black IPA, Queen Red ale and Bishop blonde as its first beers. With a crest featuring a lion with a crown, we assume the names of the beers will revolve around decks of cards. Black & Red plans on recycling all its waste, including water and spent grains. Its sustainable focus and traditional styles are sure to fit in the Austin beer scene.

Moonlight Tower Brewing Company

Moonlight Tower Brewing will be 100 percent organic. The name for the brewery was inspired by a run and the historic Austin Moontowers. All of its seven beers are brewed with organic hops and malts. As Austin loves anything organic, we are sure that the beer from Moonlight Tower Brewing will be snapped up.

R&R Brewing Company

R&R Brewing Co. will launch having already won over a dozen medals at beer competitions. After having a successful homebrewing career, R&R will be starting with American-style, small-batch beers. It is striving to buy as locally as possible and will follow the Austin brewery model by giving its spent grain to local farmers. R&R will be located in Cedar Park in Twisted X's former brewing space. The owners have also said that they might go the brewpub route and hope to open their doors in early 2014.

Strange Land Brewery

Adam Blumenshein and Tim Klatt have been building Strange Land Brewing since fall 2012. They have been working on the concept for the last three years. Located in West Lake Hills, Strange Land will be brewing out of an unused Hat Creek building. Located behind the Hat Creek Burgers, Strange Land will act like a bar and plans on having eight mainstay brews. The brewery will have a twenty-barrel system, an upgrade from its current five-gallon system. They also plan on distributing to surrounding stores. Strange Land should be open by the fall of 2013.

Solid Rock Brewing

Curt Webber, Stephen "Beaker" McCarthy and Steve Jones are opening Solid Rock Brewing off Bee Caves in West Austin. While they are in the process of building their facility, they are already putting beer on store shelves. Solid Rock plans to launch strong with seven mainstays ranging from IPAs, to vanilla milk stouts and cream ales. The brewery's owners come from all walks of life and joined forces (and skill sets) to make their dream of opening a brewery a reality. Look for them some time in 2014 in the Bee Caves area.

FUTURE SO BRIGHT WE GOTTA WEAR SHADES

The beer scene in Austin has already gained an insane amount of momentum. As the future becomes present, we are sure to see an accelerated expansion in the sheer number of breweries in the city. For every new brewery we are already hearing about, there are multiple other Austinites with a dream and a passion for brewing waiting to open the next best brewery in the capital city.

#NowFinishYourDrink

Appendix A

Glossary

ABV (alcohol by volume): the amount of alcohol measured by percentage volume of alcohol in the total volume of beer.

ABW (alcohol by weight): the amount of alcohol measured by the weight of alcohol in the total volume of beer.

aftertaste: taste left on the palate after swallowing, also referred to as the finish.

ale: beer made with a top-fermenting strain of yeast and brewed and fermented at higher temperatures.

amber: beer with an amber hue; between dark and pale.

aroma hops: hops added late in the boil to dictate the beer's bouquet or smell.

barley: cereal grain used in the malting process of fermentation.

barley wine: a strong ale with an ABV usually between 8 and 12 percent; referred to as barley wine because it is sometimes strong enough to be considered a wine but is fermented with grain instead of fruit, making it a beer.

bitch beer: any sweet malt beverage consumed in lieu of beer. Usually having an ABV of under 5 percent, bitch beers are so sweet that they are reminiscent of soda.

bite: a distinct taste of hops or acidity.

blonde: also known as golden ales, blonde ales tend to be paler in color with light body and higher carbonation.

bock: a dark and malty style of German lager. Developed in the German town of Einbeck, mispronunciations later turned the name of the beer style into "Ein Bock" and, eventually, "Bock." A traditional bock is sweet and fairly strong with an ABV of up to 7 percent.

body: a sense of fullness, or lack of it, in a beer that comes from malt and alcohol content.

bomber: a 750-milliliter bottle of beer.

bouquet: scents or smells from fermentation, often includes notes of several different scents, including fruits, grains and other plants.

brewhouse: the room or building containing brewing equipment; the place where beer is brewed.

brew kettle: vessel in which wort is boiled with hops.

brewpub: a pub or restaurant that brews and sells its own beer on the premises.

cask: barrel-shaped container for beer, usually made of wood; allows for continued fermentation of beer.

cask ale: unfiltered and unpasteurized beer that conditions in the same cask it is served from. It is also referred to as real ale.

cider: a fermented drink made with apples.

clarity: referring to the clearness of the beer, i.e., bright clarity, meaning a high level of transparency.

conditioning: aging period that allows the beer to carbonate. Cold conditioning allows for a cleaner, crisper taste, while warm conditioning allows for more complex flavors to develop.

dopplebock: a variation of a traditional bock translating as "double bock;" has a higher alcohol content and a more intense malt flavor.

draft: beer poured from a keg, tap or cask; also spelled draught.

dunkel: A dark German lager with a malty flavor created by decoction mashing, which boils some of the grains before returning them to the mash, allowing for more starches to be released. Traditionally, a dunkel has an ABV of about 5 percent and uses specialized German grains.

dunkelweizen: Not to be confused with the dunkel, the dunkleweizen is a dark wheat beer that is fruitier and sweeter.

fermentation: the conversion of sugar to acid, gases and alcohol using yeast and bacteria over the course of several weeks. The conversion results in carbon dioxide and ethyl alcohol.

firkin: a small serving vessel typically about a quarter barrel in size, typically used in cask conditioning.

flute glass: long and narrow glass used with beer to ensure that its carbonation won't dissipate; used with highly carbonated beers that have upfront aromas.

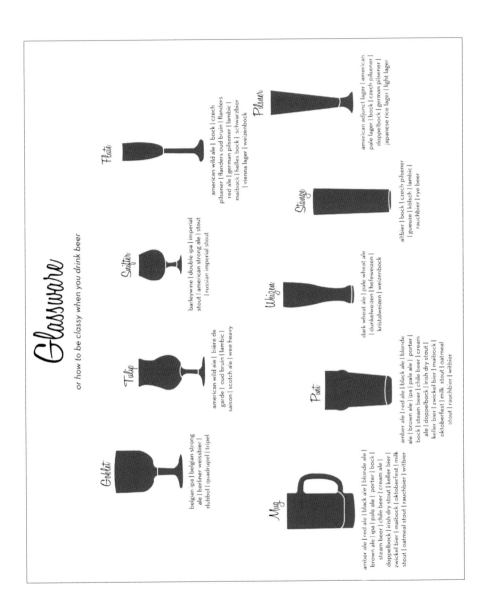

Glassware infographic. *Shaun Martin.*

fresh hopping: the addition of raw hops to the brewing process (sometimes referred to as wet hopping).

goblet: designed to maintain head on foamy beer and allow for deeper sips; traditionally used with Belgian beers.

growler: reusable container used to buy beer on site and transfer it for home consumption. Growlers are traditionally a half gallon, though it has become trendy to offer them in different sizes.

head: foam on the top of the beer.

head retention: the amount of time needed for foam on top of a poured beer to disappear.

hefe: German word for yeast; see: hefeweizen

hefeweizen: an unfiltered wheat beer with suspended wheat particles that give a cloudy appearance; traditionally possesses flavors of banana and clove.

homebrew: the process of brewing one's own beer on a small scale for personal consumption.

hoppy: a characteristic of beers that are brewed with large proportions of hops, or where the hops take on a more dominant flavor over the malt. Tastes range from floral to citric to bitter.

hops: flowers of the hop plant, the small green cones are used as a flavoring and stabilizing ingredient of beer. Hops are boiled with wort before fermentation and create a bitter taste and aroma. There are several varieties of hops in different parts of the world that create unique tastes.

IBU (international bitterness units): a system of measure to identify levels of bitterness in finished beer.

imperial stout: a strong dark beer, originally made in England to ship to Catherine II of Russia in the late 1700s; usually has a high ABV, 9 percent or higher; also referred to as Russian imperial.

India pale ale: beer style within the pale ale category that was originally brewed in England for export to India. The IPA is characterized by its intense hoppy taste.

keg: a half barrel, or 15.5 U.S. gallons.

lacing: refers to the patterns in foam or residue which stick on the inside walls of a beer glass. Typically, lacing will be more prevalent on a clean glass.

lager: a category of beer that is fermented and conditioned at low temperatures. The lager ranges in color from light to dark and has several taste variations, though it is typically lighter in taste than an ale.

malt: the foundation ingredient in beer; barley is soaked in water and allowed to sprout, and is then used to convert starch to sugars.

malt liquor: the legal name for a fermented beverage that is high in alcohol content, usually 6 percent ABV or higher.

maltose: the sugar in malt. This sugar is then converted to ethyl alcohol and carbon dioxide during the fermentation process.

malty: a characteristic of beers that are brewed with larger proportions of malts or that are brewed with more influential malt flavors. Tastes can be sweet, rich and dark.

mash: as a verb, mash is the action of releasing maltose by soaking grains in water. As a noun, mash refers to the combined mixture of grains and water.

microbrewery: a small-scale brewery that produces less than fifteen thousand barrels a year.

mouthfeel: tasting term to describe the texture of beer once it is in the mouth; i.e., beers can feel thick or thin on the tongue. Some descriptive words include smooth, creamy, slick and clean.

mug: heavy glasses with a handle and wide lip; used to hold large amounts of beer in most varieties and ideal for toasting due to their durability.

noble hops: traditional European hops used for their distinct flavor; they are typically low in bitterness and high in aroma. Examples include Hallertau, Tettnanger, Spalt and Saaz.

nose: another term for aroma or bouquet of beer.

oast house: facility used to store and dry hops after picking.

overtones: obvious tastes and characteristics in beer.

pilsner: type of pale lager, usually golden in color and fermented at relatively low temperatures.

pilsner glass: tall, tapered glass used to show color and clarity while preserving carbonation. Often used with pilsners and lagers.

pint glass: cylindrical glass, often seen in commercial use, that holds sixteen ounces of beer. The nonic pint holds twenty ounces and has a bulge near the top that allows for a better grip; used for most varieties of beer.

pony keg: a half-keg, or 7.75 U.S. gallons.

porter: a dark brown beer characterized by the use of brown malts. Often confused with the stout, the porter is generally lower in alcohol content, with an ABV of about 6 percent.

Prohibition: the banning of production, importation, sale and transportation of alcohol put forth by the Eighteenth Amendment to the U.S. Constitution in 1920. Was repealed thirteen years later by the Twenty-first Amendment.

saison: French for "season"; a highly carbonated beer with a fruity flavor, often brewed with additional spices such as ginger, coriander and orange zest. Saisons are typically light bodied with a moderate alcohol content.

schooner: an almost comically large glass, usually identified by its large, wide bowl. The schooner glass can be used to hold most kinds of beers but has traditionally been used for German wheat beers.

Scotch ale: a strong ale characterized by a sweet, caramelized taste with a bittersweet finish and a high ABV.

session beer: any beer that contains no higher than 5 percent ABV; exists so drinkers can enjoy several beers in a reasonable amount of time without reaching extreme levels of intoxication.

snifter: traditionally used with brandy and cognac, these glasses have a short stem, a wide bowl and a tapered mouth to allow for swirling to release a beer's aroma; often used with higher ABV beers such as barley wine, strong ales and imperial stouts.

sour ale: a beer style that is made to be particularly acidic by allowing wild yeast strains and souring bacteria to enter the brewing process.

specific gravity: used to determine the amount of sugars in wort; compares the density of water to the density of solid ingredients.

stout: beer made with roasted malt or barley in the brewing process. Typically a stronger version of the porter, stouts are usually dark beers but come in several variations, including blonde and imperial, along with flavors, such as chocolate, oatmeal and coffee; see: imperial stout.

taster glass: smaller glasses similar in shape to the nonic pint glass. These glasses usually hold about four ounces and are used to give samples of a wide variety of beers.

tulip: tulip-shaped glass used to hold beers with foamy heads; often used with Scotch ales, saisons and Belgian beers.

undertone: subtle tastes and scents.

vinous: referring to tastes and scents in wine, usually found in high ABV beers.

weizen glass: tall glass that widens near the top to capture foamier heads often found in wheat beers, hence the name.

wheat beer: beer that is made with a large amount of wheat in addition to barley.

wort: the solution of malt sugars strained from the grains and used in fermentation to produce beer.

yeast: a microorganism in the Fungi kingdom used in fermentation to create carbon dioxide and alcohol. Yeast can come in different strains. Top-fermenting yeast strains are used in ale-type beer production while bottom-fermenting strains are used in lager-type beer.

zymurgy: study of chemistry relating to the fermentation process.

Appendix B

Breweries, Brewpubs, Craft Beer Bars and Bottle Shops

Breweries

Adelbert's Brewery
2314 Rutland Drive Suite 100

Austin Beerworks
3009 Industrial Terrace

Circle Brewing Company
2340 West Braker Lane

(512) Brewing
407 Radam Lane

Independence Brewing Company
3913 Todd Lane

Live Oak Brewing Company
3301 East Fifth Street

Real Ale Brewing Company
231 San Saba Court

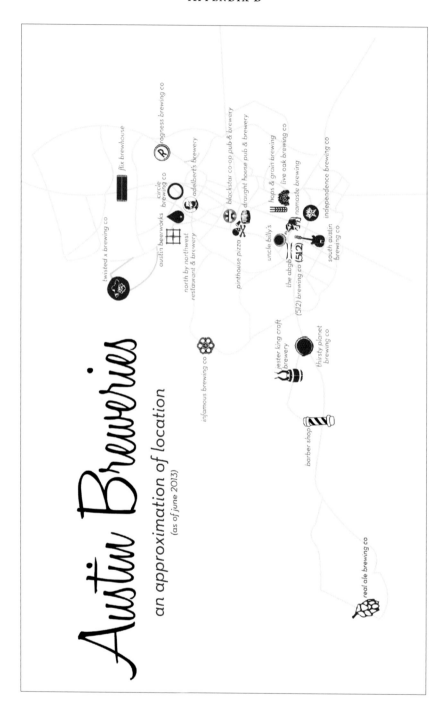

Brewery map infographic. *Shaun Martin.*

Rogness Brewing Company
2400 Patterson Industrial Drive
Pflugerville, Texas 78660

South Austin Brewing Company
415 East Street Elmo Road

Thirsty Planet Brewing Company
11160 Circle Drive

Twisted X Brewing Company
3200 Woodall Drive C1

BREWPUBS

The Austin Brew Garden and Brewing Co. (ABGB)
1305 West Oltorf

The Barber Shop
207 West Mercer Street
Dripping Springs, Texas 78620

Black Star Co-op
7020 Easy Wind Drive Suite 100

Draught House Pub and Brewery
4112 Medical Parkway

Flix Brewhouse
2200 South Interstate 35 B1
Round Rock, Texas 78681

Hops & Grain
507 Calles Street

Infamous Brewing
4602 Weletka Drive

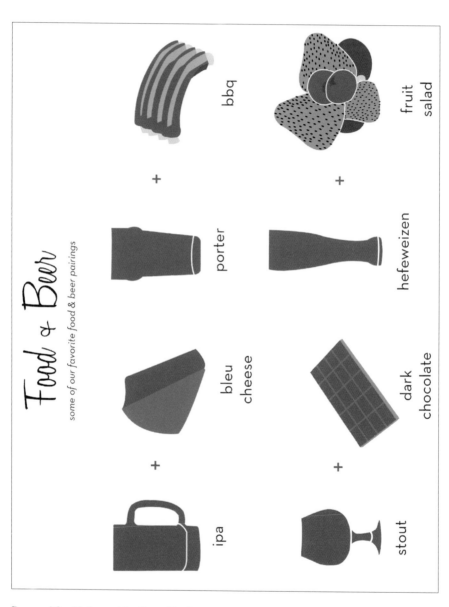

Beer and food infographic. *Shaun Martin.*

Jester King Craft Brewing
13005 Fitzhugh Road

Namaste Brewing
1950 North Interstate 35 Frontage Road

North by Northwest Restaurant and Brewery
10010 North Capital of Texas Highway

Pinthouse Pizza
4729 Burnet Road

Uncle Billy's Brew and Que
1530 Barton Springs Road

CRAFT BEER BARS

Austin Ale House
310 East Sixth Street

Banger's Sausage House and Beer Garden
79 Rainey Street

The Barber Shop
207 West Mercer Street
Dripping Springs, Texas 78620

Billy's on Burnet
2105 Hancock Drive

The Black Heart
86 Rainey Street

Black Sheep Lodge
2108 South Lamar Boulevard

Black Star Co-op
7020 Easy Wind Drive Suite 100

The Brass Tap
204 East Main Street
Round Rock, Texas 78664

Brew Exchange
706 West Sixth Street

Chicago House
607 Trinity Street

Craft Pride
61 Rainey Street

Dig Pub
401 Cypress Creek Road
Cedar Park, Texas 78613

Dog & Duck Pub
406 West Seventeenth Street

Drink.Well
207 East Fifty-third Street

Easy Tiger
709 East Sixth Street

G&S Lounge
2420 South First Street

The Ginger Man
301 Lavaca Street

Glass Half Full Taproom
14028 North U.S. Highway 183, Building F

The Grackle
1700 East Sixth Street

HandleBar
121 East Fifth Street

Hi Hat Public House
2121 East Sixth Street

Homefield Grill
2000 North Interstate 35 Frontage Road
Round Rock, Texas 78681

Hopfields
3110 Guadalupe Street

Icenhauer's
83 Rainey Street

Liberty Bar
1618½ East Sixth Street

Opal Divine's
3601 South Congress Avenue

Quickie Pickie
1208 East Eleventh Street

Red's Porch
3508 South Lamar Boulevard

The Tavern
922 West Twelfth Street

Westside Alehouse
1500 North Interstate 35 Frontage Road
Round Rock, Texas 78681

Whip In
1950 North Interstate 35 Frontage Road

Workhorse Bar
100 North Loop Boulevard East

Yellow Jacket Social Club
1704 East Fifth Street

Bottle Shops

Antonelli's Cheese Shop
4220 Duval Street

Barton Hill's Food Mart
2900 South Lamar Boulevard

Central Market
4001 North Lamar Boulevard
4477 South Lamar Boulevard

Craft Pride
61 Rainey Street

East 1st Grocery
1811 East Cesar Chavez Street

Growler Room
6800 Burnet Road, Suite 2

Henri's Cheese and Wine
2026 South Lamar Boulevard

Hyde Park Market
4429 Duval Street

Junior's Beer & Wine
705 West Twenty-ninth Street

King Liquor
5310 Burnet Road

Live Oak Market
4410 Manchaca Road

MLK Food Store
2915 East Martin Luther King Jr. Boulevard

Quickie Pickie
1208 East Eleventh Street

River City Market
2209 South Congress Avenue

Rosedale Market
1309 West Forty-fifth Street

Royal Blue Market
247 West Third Street
360 Nueces Street

South Lamar Wine and Spirits
2418 South Lamar Boulevard

Spec's Wine, Spirits and Finer Food
4970 West Highway 290
5775 Airport Boulevard
10601 Ranch Road 620 North
13015 Shops Parkway

Sunrise MiniMart
1809 West Anderson Lane

Tejas Liquor #2
2113 Wells Branch Parkway, Suite 700

Whip In
1950 North Interstate 35 Frontage Road

Whole Foods
1105 North Lamar Boulevard, Suite 200
9607 Research Boulevard
4301 West William Cannon Drive, Suite 800

World Market
5601 Brodie Lane

Appendix C

Day Trips

Dripping Springs

The gateway to the Hill Country, the Dripping Springs area has quickly become a destination for great craft beer (and a convenient one at that, it's only 25 miles from Austin). With two breweries each growing more popular by the day nearby, it's easy to spend the day wandering the grounds at Jester King or on a stool in the air conditioning at Thirsty Planet. Or if you'd rather not commit to one brewery, head a few miles down the road to the Barbershop for a great selection of Austin beers, including their own creations.

San Antonio

While it's important to remember the Alamo, it's also important to remember to drink local. Luckily, if you're in San Antonio, that shouldn't be too hard. About 80 miles from Austin, Ranger Creek (4834 Whirlwind Street, San Antonio, Texas 78217) is a brewery and distillery offering not only beer but also the whiskey chaser to go with it. But if you're not into whiskey, you can go try some small-batch beer at Freetail Brewing (4035 North Loop 1604 West, Suite 105, San Antonio, Texas 78257) or a variety of internationally inspired beers over at Blue Star Brewing (1414 South Alamo Street, Suite

105, San Antonio, Texas 78210). Also, Freetail and Blue Star both are both brewpubs, so you won't have to drink on an empty stomach.

WIMBERLEY

Less than an hour outside Austin, Wimberley is a quick getaway from the Austin traffic and a great place to try some new beers. Open since 2011, Middleton Brewing and Home Brew (Ranch Road 12 Wimberley, Texas 78666) hosts a number of tastings and beer classes each month. But if you'd rather not do that much work, there's a number of mainstays and rotating taps to sit back and enjoy.

FREDERICKSBURG

While Fredericksburg is known to most as wine country, the town has been known to pour a few beers as well. The Fredericksburg Brewing Company (245 East Main Street Fredericksburg, Texas 78624) has a large biergarten for events as well as a rotating tap of cleverly named beers, such as the Not-So-Dumb Blonde. And if you don't feel like driving 80 miles home after all that beer and wine, you're in luck, because the brewery is also a bed-and-brew—that's right, a bed-and-breakfast/brewery. The hotel offers a sampler flight to each overnight guest, in case you needed extra incentive.

NEW BRAUNFELS

Schlitterbahn isn't the only attraction in New Braunfels. If you're looking for a more laid-back vacation, there are a variety of places to visit for the twenty-one-and-up crowd. 50 miles south of Austin, it's home to the oldest dance hall in Texas, Gruene, which now serves as a country music concert venue. And since it can't hurt to have a bit of liquid courage before attempting that two-step, there are plenty of saloons and brewery taprooms to wet your whistle in:

Gruene Hall: 1281 Gruene Road, New Braunfels, Texas 78130
Phoenix Saloon: 193 West San Antonio Street, New Braunfels, Texas 78130
Faust Brewing Co.: 240 South Seguin Avenue, New Braunfels, Texas 78130
Guadalupe Brewing: 1580 Wald Road, Suite 1, New Braunfels, Texas, 78132
New Braunfels Brewing Co.: 180 West Mill Street, New Braunfels, Texas, 78130

Round Rock/Pflugerville

Located on the outskirts of Austin, the cities of Pflugerville and Round Rock are just a quick trip 20 miles north on I-35 for plenty of shopping, restaurants and, of course, lots of craft beer. Here, you can find Flix Brewhouse, the world's first (and only) first-run movie theater with an in-house brewery. After the movie, head over to Rogness Brewing for an afternoon tasting or one of its monthly game nights.

Shiner

About 80 miles from Austin, between Houston and San Antonio, is the city of Shiner and the location of Spoetzl Brewing (603 East Brewery Street, Shiner, Texas 77984), one of the oldest still-standing breweries in Texas. Known for its widely distributed Shiner Bock, Spoetzl Brewing is also famous for using Texas ingredients, such as pecans, peaches and ruby red grapefruits.

Bibliography

Abendschein, Matt. Interview with Arianna Auber. June 3, 2013.

Accum, Friedrich Christian. *A Treatise on Adulterations of Food and Culinary Poisons*…London: printed by J. Mallett and sold by Longman, Hurst, Rees, Orme, and Brown, 1820.

Airheart, Jon. Interview with Caroline Wallace. March 20, 2013.

Alan, David. "A 'Craft' Course in Texas Beer." *L Style G Style*. http://www.lstylegstyle.com/archive/imbibe/a-craft-course-in-texas-beer/ (accessed June 30, 2013).

Anchor Brewing. "Anchor Steam." http://www.anchorbrewing.com/beer/anchor_steam (accessed May 17, 2013).

Anderson, Steve. Interview by Wendy Cawthon. June 24, 2013.

Austin Board of Trade. *The Industrial Advantages of Austin, Texas; or, Austin Up To Date*. Austin, TX: Akehurst Publishing Co., 1894. Digital images from Portal to Texas History, University of North Texas Libraries. Original from Austin History Center, Austin Public Library, Austin, TX. http://texashistory.unt.edu/ark:/67531/metapth38097/ (accessed June 23, 2013).

Austin Chronicle. "Lovejoys." November 14, 1997. http://www.austinchronicle.com/food/1997-11-14/518890 (accessed May 13, 2013).

———. "Texas on Tap." November 3, 1995. http://www.austinchronicle.com/food/1995-11-03/529982/ (accessed April 18, 2013).

———. "The Waterloo Brewing Company & American Grill." November 14, 1997. http://www.austinchronicle.com/food/1997-11-14/518892/ (accessed May 13, 2013).

Austin Texas June 1877. New York: Sanborn Map & Publishing Co., 1877. Texas and Mexico Sanborn Maps 1877–1922. Perry-Castañeda Map Collection. University of Texas Library. http://www.lib.utexas.edu/maps/sanborn/txu-sanborn-austin-1877-1.jpg (accessed March 5, 2013).

Austin Texas June 1885. New York: Sanborn Map & Publishing Co., 1885. Texas and Mexico Sanborn Maps 1877–1922. Perry-Castañeda Map Collection. University of Texas Library. http://www.lib.utexas.edu/maps/sanborn/txu-sanborn-austin-1885-1.jpg (accessed March 5, 2013).

Barr, Andrew. *Drink: A Social History of America*. New York: Carroll & Graf Publishers, Inc. 1999.

Bearden, William. Interview by Arianna Auber. April 17, 2013.

Beer Advocate. "Beer and Brewing Terms." http://beeradvocate.com/beer/101/terms.php (accessed March 23, 2013).

Black & Red Brewing Co. http://blackandredbrewing.com/ (accessed June 27, 2013).

Booth, Chris. Interview by Arianna Auber. May 17, 2013.

Bordeau, Shane. Interview by Holly Aker. June 7, 2013.

Bradley, Keith. Interview by Caroline Wallace. June 12, 2013.

Bradley, Pam. Interview by Caroline Wallace. June 12, 2013.

Brand, Kevin. Interview by Sarah Wood. June 21, 2013.

Buchanan, Larry, and Daniel Fromson. "Mapping the Rise of Craft Beer." Idea of the Week. *New Yorker*, June 7, 2013. http://www.newyorker.com/sandbox/business/beer.html (accessed June 27, 2013).

Bush Baby Beer. "About Bush Baby Beer." http://bushbabybeer.com/about/ (accessed June 27, 2013).

Cartwright, Amy. Interview by Sarah Wood. June 14, 2013.

———. Interview by Arianna Auber. June 14, 2013.

Cartwright, Gary. "Beer Brawl." *Texas Monthly* (April 1993).

———. "Crazy for Brew." *Texas Monthly* (November 1995).

Celis, Christine. Interview by Caroline Wallace. June 26, 2013.

Cerda, Debbie. Interview by Caroline Wallace. June 6, 2013.

Chamberlain, Aaron. Interview by Arianna Auber. June 20, 2013.

"Charles William Pressler (Carl Wilhelm Pressler) and Clara Johanna Doerk Pressler." Herman Pressler Biography File. Austin History Center.

Clark, Forrest, Patrick Clark, and Marco Rodriguez. Interview by Shaun Martin. June 2, 2013.

Cooney, Aoibhistin, Benjamin Yiapan, Brio Yiapan, and Mushahidi Ole Yiapan. Interview with Shaun Martin. June 19, 2013.

Crocker, Ronnie. "Updated: Beer Bills Become Law." *Houston Chronicle*, 14 June 2013. http://blog.chron.com/beertx/2013/06/beer-bills-set-to-become-law (accessed June 24, 2013).

Curry, W.M., ed. *Crosbyton (TX) Review* 19, no. 19, ed. 1. May 27, 1927. Digital images from Portal to Texas History, University of North Texas Libraries. Original from Crosby County Public Library, Crosbyton, TX. http://texashistory.unt.edu/ark:/67531/metapth255674 (accessed June 25, 2013).

DeBower, Adam. Interview by Holly Aker. June 25, 2013.

Dewberry, Dan. Interview by Caroline Wallace. May 21, 2013.

Dobies, J.M. "Mistake by the Lake: Last call at Uncle Billy's." *Examiner.com*, November 12, 2012. http://www.examiner.com/article/mistake-by-the-lake-last-call-at-uncle-billy-s (June 30, 2013).

Ebel, Dave. Interview by Caroline Wallace. June 11, 2013.

Ebel, Melissa. Interview by Caroline Wallace. June 11, 2013.

Ellison Photo Co. Falstaff Beer Trucks. May 25, 1934. Digital image from Portal to Texas History, University of North Texas Libraries. Original from Austin History Center, Austin Pubic Library, Austin, TX. http://texashistory.unt.edu/ark:/67531/metapth125330/ (accessed June 30, 2013).

Encyclopædia Britannica Online. "Eighteenth Amendment." http://www.britannica.com/EBchecked/topic/181228/Eighteenth-Amendment (accessed June 23, 2013).

Encyclopedia Mythica. "Ninkasi." http://www.pantheon.org/articles/n/ninkasi.html (accessed June 23, 2013).

Feit, Rachel. "Gardens of Eden: How Austin Used to Celebrate." *Austin Chronicle*, January 26, 2001.

Fowler, Tom. "Great Grains Picks Up Austin Brewing Contract." *Dallas Business Journal*, July 9, 1999. http://www.accessmylibrary.com/article-1G1-55329660/great-grains-picks-up.html (accessed June 30, 2013).

Golden, William. Interview by Holly Aker. June 25, 2013.

Graham, Michael. Interview by Holly Aker. June 25, 2013.

Gray, S.A. *Mercantile and General City Directory of Austin, Texas, 1872–1873*. 1872. Digital images from Portal to Texas History, University of North Texas Libraries. Originals from Austin History Center, Austin Public Library, Austin, TX. http://texashistory.unt.edu/ark:/67531/metapth38126/ (accessed June 23, 2013).

Griffin, Dariush, and John Stecker. Interview by Shaun Martin. June 19, 2013.

Hare, Josh. Interview by Holly Aker. April 17, 2013.

Haworth, Alan Lee. "Threadgill, John Kenneth." *Handbook of Texas Online*. Texas State Historical Association. http://www.tshaonline.org/handbook/online/articles/fth58 (accessed July 13, 2013).

Hazelwood, Claudia. "Waterloo, TX (Travis County)." *Handbook of Texas Online*. Texas State Historical Association. http://www.tshaonline.org/handbook/online/articles/hvw13 (accessed June 23, 2013).

Hennech, Mike. *Encyclopedia of Texas Breweries: Pre-Prohibition (1836–1918)*. Irving, TX: Ale Publishing, 1990.

Hennech, Michael C., and Tracé Etienne-Gray. "Brewing Industry." *Handbook of Texas Online*. Texas State Historical Association. http://www.tshaonline.org/handbook/online/articles/dib01 (accessed June 23, 2013).

Holt, Jeff. "Austin." TexasBreweries.com. http://www.texasbreweries.com/index.html (accessed March 16, 2013).

Horowitz, Josh. Interview by Holly Aker. June 25, 2013.

House of Representatives. H.R.1337, 1977. Washington DC, Rep Steiger, William A., 1978.

Hovey, Scott. "Adelbert's Brewery." Episode nine of the *Beer Diaries*. http://www.thebeerdiaries.tv/episodes/9-adelberts-brewery/ (accessed June 16, 2013).

Humphrey, David C. "Austin, TX (Travis County)." *Handbook of Texas Online*. Texas State Historical Association. http://www.tshaonline.org/handbook/online/articles/hda03 (accessed July 23, 2013).

Jensen, Mark. Interview by Shaun Martin. May 30, 2013.

Jester King Brewery. "The Change in Texas Beer Law & What it Means for Us." http://jesterkingbrewery.com/the-change-in-texas-beer-law-what-it-means-for-us (accessed June 25, 2013).

Johnson, Julie. "Pull Up a Stool with Chip McElroy." *All About Beer Magazine* (March 2011). http://allaboutbeer.com/live-beer/people/pull-up-a-stool/2011/03/with-chip-mcelroy/ (accessed June 15, 2013).

Johnson, Pableaux. "Austin's Brewpub Bargains." *Austin Chronicle*, July 19, 1996. http://www.austinchronicle.com/food/1996-07-19/532160/ (accessed March 16, 2013).

———. "Glass of '93: Five Years of Austin Brewpubs." *Austin Chronicle*, April 24, 1998. http://www.austinchronicle.com/food/1998-04-24/523331 (accessed June 30, 2013).

Kerr, K. Austin. "Prohibition." *Handbook of Texas Online*. Texas State Historical Association. http://www.tshaonline.org/handbook/online/articles/vap01 (accessed June 25, 2013).

Lerner, Mason. "Beer, Breweries and Science." *Houston Chronicle*, January 5, 2007. http://www.chron.com/news/article/Beer-breweries-and-science-1793645.php (accessed March 23 2013).

Maddux, Jake. Interview by Arianna Auber. May 5, 2013.

Marshall, John, ed. *State Gazette (Austin, TX)* 11, no. 36, ed. 1. April 14, 1860. Digital images from Portal to Texas History, University of North Texas Libraries. Originals from Dolph Briscoe Center for American History, Austin, TX. http://texashistory.unt.edu/ark:/67531/metapth81429/ (accessed June 23, 2013.

Marshall, Webb. "Review: North by Northwest Restaurant & Brewery." *Austin Chronicle*, July 6, 2007, http://www.austinchronicle.com/food/2007-07-06/499206 (accessed June 10, 2013).

Martin, Angela. Interview by Caroline Wallace. June 5, 2013.

Martin, Corey. Interview by Caroline Wallace. June 5, 2013.

McElroy, Chip. Interview by Kat McCullough. June 28, 2013.

McGinnis, Matt. "Austin's Top Draft Picks." *Austin Man Magazine* (Fall 2012). http://www.atxman.com/austins-top-draft-picks (accessed June 30, 2013).

McGovern, Mike. Interview by Holly Aker. June 25, 2013.

Moffatt, Lori. "Cheers to Texas Craft Breweries." *Texas Highways* (August 1995).

Mohrfeld, Joe. Interview by Arianna Auber. March 23, 2013.

———. Interview by Caroline Wallace. October 2012.

———. Interview by Holly Aker. June 29, 2013.

Mooney & Morrison. *Mooney & Morrison's General Directory of the City of Austin, Texas, for 1877–78.* 1877. Digital images from Portal to Texas History, University of North Texas Libraries. Originals from Austin History Center, Austin Public Library, Austin, Texas. http://texashistory.unt.edu/ark:/67531/metapth46838/ (accessed June 23, 2013).

Moonlight Tower Brewing Company. "About Moonlight Tower Brewing." http://moonlighttowerbrewing.com/about/ (accessed June 27, 2013).

Morrison & Fourmy Directory Co. *Morrison & Fourmy's General Directory of the City of Austin for 1881–1882.* 1881. Digital images from Portal to Texas History, University of North Texas Libraries. Originals from Austin History Center, Austin Public Library, Austin, Texas. http://texashistory.unt.edu/ark:/67531/metapth39151/ (accessed June 23, 2013).

———. *Morrison & Fourmy's General Directory of the City of Austin for 1885–86.* 1885. Digital images from Portal to Texas History, University of North Texas Libraries. Originals from Austin History Center, Austin Public Library, Austin, Texas. http://texashistory.unt.edu/ark:/67531/metapth46837/ (accessed June 23, 2013).

————. *Morrison & Fourmy's General Directory of the City of Austin for 1900–1901*. 1900. Digital images from Portal to Texas History, University of North Texas Libraries. Originals from Austin History Center, Austin Public Library, Austin, Texas. http://texashistory.unt.edu/ark:/67531/metapth61100/ (accessed June 23, 2013).

Murff, Billy. Interview by Sarah Wood. April 25, 2013.

Myers, Cindi. "What's Brewing at the Pub?" *Texas Highways* (August 1995).

"New Microbrewery Makes Austin Debut." *Free Library* (March 2). http://www.thefreelibrary.com/New microbrewery makes Austin debut.-a012120073 (accessed June 30, 2013).

News 8 Austin Staff. "Bitter End Restaurant Catches Fire." *YNN Austin*. Modified August 22, 2005. http://austin.ynn.com/content/top_stories/143811/bitter-end-restaurant-catches-fire (accessed June 12, 2013).

Night, Bill, "The Draught House, Austin." *It's Pub Night*, March 17, 2008. http://www.its-pub-night.com/2008/03/draught-house-austin.html (accessed June 4, 2013).

NXNW. "About NXNW." http://nxnwbrew.com/about/about_nxnw (accessed June 22, 2013).

Oglesby, Chris. Interview by Holly Aker. June 17, 2013.

Orf, Chris. Interview by Shaun Martin. June 5, 2013.

"Paul Pressler (1835–1894)." Ancestry.com. http://records.ancestry.com/Paul_Pressler_records.ashx?pid=162716341 (accessed May 16, 2013).

PBS. "Prohibition in the Borderlands." http://texaspbs.org/texas-programming/prohibition-in-the-borderland/ (accessed April 15, 2013).

Peters, Brian. Interview by Caroline Wallace. June 10, 2013.

Pope, Colin. "Sixth Street's Copper Tank Closes, Selling Brewing Equipment." *Austin Business Journal*, March 6, 2005. http://www.bizjournals.com/austin/stories/2005/03/07/story5.html?page=all (accessed June 30, 2013).

Prewitt, Cary. Interview by Shaun Martin. June 5, 2013.

Quigley, Ian. "The Fantastic and Utterly Disreputable History of the Bevy of Sin Known as Guy Town: Before It Was the Warehouse District, It Was the Whorehouse District." *Austin Chronicle*, January 26, 2001. http://www.austinchronicle.com/features/2001-01-26/80321 (accessed April 3, 2013).

R&R Brewing Company. https://www.facebook.com/pages/RR-Brewing-company/136646119846094?ref=stream (accessed June 27, 2013).

"Real Ale." Episode five of the *Beer Diaries*. http://www.thebeerdiaries.tv/episodes/5-real-ale/ (accessed June 16, 2013).

Rice, Rachel. "Hat Creek Burgers to Partner with New Brewery." *Austin American-Statesman.* May 29, 2013. http://www.statesman.com/news/news/local/hat-creek-burgers-to-partner-with-new-brewery/nX6LH/ (accessed June 24, 2013).

Rinehart, Andrew. Interview by Shaun Martin. June 23, 2013.

Rizza, Justin. Interview by Holly Aker. June 20, 2013.

Rogness, Forrest. Interview by Holly Aker and Caroline Wallace. May 29, 2013.

Sabel, Ben. Interview by Sarah Wood. June 19, 2013.

Sampson, Jim. Interview by Holly Aker. June 7, 2013.

Scholz Garten. "August Scholz." http://www.scholzgarten.net/scholz_history_new-august.html (accessed March 19, 2013).

Schoppe, Mark. Interview by Caroline Wallace. June 11, 2013.

Severson, Amy. "Dallas History, Dry America (1931, Cokesbury Press)." *Dallas Cook Book.* http://thedallascookbook.blogspot.com/2008/08/dallas-history-dry-america-1931.html (accessed May 1, 2013).

Smittle, Brian. "Thirsty Planet Brewing Company." Episode two of *Beer Diaries.* http://www.thebeerdiaries.tv/episodes/2-thirsty-planet-brewing-company/ (accessed June 16, 2013).

Smittle, Brian, and Ben Sabin. Interview by Sarah Wood. June 24, 2013.

Smoot, Lawrence K. O. *Henry's Wedding.* N.d. Digital images from Portal to Texas History, University of North Texas Libraries. Originals from Austin History Center, Austin Public Library, Austin, Texas. http://texashistory.unt.edu/ark:/67531/metapth139271/ (accessed June 23, 2013).

Sprague, Leslie. Interview by Arianna Auber. May 1, 2013.

Strange Land Brewery. http://www.strangelandbrewery.com (accessed June 27, 2013).

Stuffings, Jeffery. Interview by Holly Aker. May 18, 2013.

Sutton, Jared Paul. *Ethnic Minorities and Prohibition in Texas, 1887 to 1919.* UNT Digital Library. Denton, Texas. http://digital.library.unt.edu/ark:/67531/metadc5341/ (accessed June 25, 2013).

Sykes, Kevin. Interview by Holly Aker. June 18, 2013.

Tait, Chip. Interview by Kat McCullough. June 20, 2013.

Texas Alcoholic Beverage Commission. "Alcoholic Beverage Code." Statute Title 4. Chapter 109. Subchapter B. §109.21. Austin, TX, 1977.

Texas Almanac. "Prohibition Elections in Texas." http://www.texasalmanac.com/topics/elections/prohibition-elections-texas (accessed May 12, 2013).

Texas State Library and Archives Commission. "Votes for Women! The Movement Comes of Age." https://www.tsl.state.tx.us/exhibits/suffrage/comesofage/page1.html (accessed April 25, 2013).

Triple XXX Brewing. "Our Root Beer Has a History We're Proud of." http://www.triplexxxrootbeer.com/history.html (accessed May 15, 2013).

Troutman, Chris. Interview by Arianna Auber. June 20, 2013.

Tucker, Davis. Interview by Kat McCullough. June 20, 2013.

"U.S. Border Patrol with Confiscated Liquor." N.d. Digital images from Portal to Texas History, University of North Texas Libraries. Originals from Marfa Public Library, Marfa, TX. http://texashistory.unt.edu/ark:/67531/metapth87534/ (accessed June 25, 2013).

Valhonrat, Charles. Interview by Arianna Auber. June 10, 2013.

Various. "From Information Submitted for Historical Marker." In *Flour House Documentation*. Austin: Texas Historical Commission, 2009.

W., Adele. Interview by Mattie L. Seymore. *Frederick William Sutor*. Austin History Center, June 23, 1964.

Waters, Michael. Interview by Sarah Wood. June 14, 2013.

Weeks, Jordan. Interview by Holly Aker. June 17, 2013.

White, Joe. Interview by Caroline Wallace. June 17, 2013.

Wilson, Josh. Interview by Kat McCullough. June 25, 2013.

Wolosin, Ty. Interview by Holly Aker. June 18, 2013.

Young, Jeff. Interview by Sarah Wood. April 30, 2013.

Index

About BitchBeer.org

S tarted in February 2012, BitchBeer.org is a blog that reclaims the term "bitch beer," which is often used to describe low-calorie, low-alcohol content beverages that are marketed to serve as the female counterpart for beer, a stereotypical "male" drink. From covering the Great American Beer Festival in Denver to trying all the latest and greatest releases from local Austin breweries, *Bitch Beer*'s mission is to prove that any beer can be "bitch beer" and that women can be just as passionate about craft beer as men. The blog strives to bring beer news, features and a little feminism to the Texas craft beer community. *Bitch Beer* has been named one of the "Top 10 Austin Food Blogs" by the *Austin Chronicle* and has been featured in a number of other publications, including *Austin Monthly*, *Austin Woman* magazine and the *Austin Post*. Stepping away from the glow of a computer monitor, the women of *Bitch Beer* have appeared on several podcasts, web series and television spots, including Cooking Channel's *Food Fanatics*, PBS's *Food Finder*, the *Beer Diaries*, Bake Space's *Kitchen Party* and the *Beerists* podcast. They have also spoken at a variety of public events, including the TechMunch Food Bloggers' Conference and the Austin History Center's Beer Garden Social: A Nineteenth-century Family Experience. *Austin Beer: Capital City History on Tap* is a collaborative effort among the authors of the blog. For more from them, visit www.bitchbeer.org.

About the Authors

From left to right: Wendy Cawthon, Kat McCullough, Holly Aker, Sarah Wood, Shaun Martin, Caroline Wallace and Arianna Auber. *Juan Carlos Ferrer.*

HOLLY AKER

Holly's first introduction to beer was at the age of sixteen, when she and her friends began stealing their parents' Busch Camo. She quickly learned the error of her ways after attending the Off-Centered Film Fest when she was twenty-one and fell in love with craft beer and the community. As an English writing and rhetoric major at St. Edward's University, Holly got the question, "So what? You want to write a book?" a lot. And every time her answer was a sharp, "Hell no! Never." Well, if you've reached this point in this book, you know that obviously changed. She's spoken about craft beer at events such as the TechMunch Food Bloggers Conference, "Kitchen Party" and PBS's *Food Finder*. She now crushes it daily as an SEO/marketing professional, die-hard Dallas Cowboys fan and drinker of only the finest craft brews.

ARIANNA AUBER

Arianna (or Ari, as her friends call her) started drinking beer once she realized it didn't all taste like watery Budweiser. One of her proudest moments was the lunch her mom decided to order a Live Oak HefeWeizen, instead of a Dos Equis, and enjoyed it, although Arianna's go-to pint will always be a (512) Pecan Porter (and just about any other porter). She's spoken about her love for beer on PBS's *Food Finder* show with the other Bitch Beer girls. A crime show junkie, she is a staff writer with the *Austin American-Statesman* who reports on events and interesting people in Texas's capital city, a job that has shown her, over and over, the determined, entrepreneurial spirit just about every driven Austinite—including many local craft brewers—has in spades.

WENDY CAWTHON

Wendy is a connoisseur of fine-ish cheeses, wines, tequilas and craft beers, proving that bitches aren't limited to low-cal cocktails. One of her favorite pastimes is cooking with beer, either as an ingredient or as a way to stay hydrated. A former bartender, Wendy discovered her appreciation for craft beer after serving way too many Bud Lights to customers. She enjoys lagers, golden ales and the winter seasonals that she looks forward to all year long. She currently lives in Dallas, Texas, and works as an editor.

SHAUN MARTIN

Shaun was not always a beer lover. Now she drinks anything from porters to double IPAs. Preferring sours and chili beers, Shaun is not a huge IPA or pale ale fan. Live Oak HefeWeizen changed her life, as it was the first beer that she legitimately enjoyed. She has been featured in the Cooking Channel show *Food Fanatics* and the PBS show *Food Finder*. Shaun's day job is working as a graphic designer, her first love. She now incorporates her two loves, beer and graphic design, by doing the Bitch Beer branding and occasional shirt design.

-

KAT MCCULLOUGH

Kat began her journey with beer when she forced herself to drink an entire Lone Star—and loved it. From that moment on, Kat knew she wanted to shove every beer in her path into her gullet. After trying Thirsty Planet's Pumpkin Masala, she knew that her life would be forever changed. She has been featured on Bake Space's webisode series, *Kitchen Party.* Including her interest in beer, Kat loves all things Scotland, has a cat named Charles and has a huge passion for nutrition and health.

CAROLINE WALLACE

Caroline's passion for beer blossomed at the ripe old age of nineteen, when she spent a semester abroad in Wellington, New Zealand. After an eighteen-hour plane ride, she suddenly found herself above the country's legal drinking age and surrounded by a burgeoning craft beer scene. After graduating from college back in Austin, she began to really gain an appreciation for the amazing variety of beers being produced in the capital city. Caroline has been featured as a guest on a variety of programs including the *When in Austin* and the *Beerists* podcasts and the *Beer Diaries*'s web series "Pubs, Pints and Pals." She recently gave a talk on pre-Prohibition brewing at an event sponsored by the Austin History Center. In addition to writing about beer, Caroline works in film and video production and is an incredibly novice homebrewer and lunch beer enthusiast.

SARAH WOOD

Sarah, a quality-assurance engineer at a mobile solutions firm, loves great food, a good book and an excellent beer or four. Although her boozy tastes have not always been quite so refined, she has reformed her lowbrow drinking ways and is taking the craft beer scene by the horns by never turning her nose up at a new style she might come across. Sarah plays an active role in shaping the graphic identity of Bitch Beer by contributing poster designs and illustrations for many community events and parties. She has also been featured in *Austin Monthly* and is constantly advocating for better beer choices throughout the less-educated community.

Visit us at
www.historypress.net

....

This title is also available as an e-book